Study Guide

to accompany

ROBERT **SIEGLER**

JUDY **DELOACHE**

NANCY **EISENBERG**

How Children DEVELOP
second edition

THE LEARNING CENTRE
TOWER HAMLETS COLLEGE
ARBOUR SQUARE
LONDON E1 0PS

Jill L. Saxon, Ph.D.

WORTH PUBLISHERS

KT-227-064

Order No:

Class: 155.4 SAX

Accession No: 105674

Type: L

Study Guide
by Jill L. Saxon
to accompany
Siegler, DeLoache, Eisenberg: **How Children Develop**, Second Edition

© 2006, 2003 by Worth Publishers

All rights reserved.
No part of this publication may be reproduced, stored in a retrieval system,
or transmitted in any form or by any means, electronic, mechanical,
photocopying, or otherwise, without the prior written permission
of the publisher.

ISBN: 0-7167-6720-1
EAN: 9780716767206

Printed in the United States of America

First Printing 2006

Worth Publishers
41 Madison Avenue
New York, NY 10010
www.worthpublishers.com

Contents

Preface

This Study Guide is designed for use with *How Children Develop,* second edition, by Robert Siegler, Judy DeLoache, and Nancy Eisenberg. The 16 chapters correspond to the 16 chapters in the textbook. Each chapter contains learning objectives, a review section, two key term matching sections, multiple-choice questions, and essay questions. This book is intended to help students evaluate their understanding of the textbook material and then guide them toward any problem areas that need to be reviewed.

Learning Objectives are included at the beginning of each chapter. The second section, "**You Should Know**," reminds students of the general content areas of the textbook, including both factual and conceptual issues. Rather than duplicating the summary sections located in the textbook, the "You Should Know" section helps students organize their knowledge in a series of "hows," "whys," and "whats" presented in a bullet-point style.

Each chapter also contains two **Key Term Matching sections**. Key Term Matching I allows students to test their knowledge of the key terms and their definitions in the traditional fashion. Key Term Matching II allows students to assess their knowledge of key terms with a more difficult test of concepts, by pairing key terms with appropriate applications and examples.

The **Multiple-Choice Questions** section contains 20 sample multiple-choice items that are designed to be similar in style and content to those items students will find on quizzes and exams. The questions vary as to difficulty level and test both definitional and conceptual knowledge. Some items concentrate on direct recall of information, while other items require a deeper understanding of the material and the ability to apply the concepts to real-world examples. A **True/False** section is also included.

An **Answer Key** containing answers to the two matching sections, the true/false questions, and the multiple-choice questions appears at the end of each chapter.

Finally, each chapter contains five sample **Essay Questions**, again designed to be similar in style and content to questions students may find on quizzes and exams. The essay questions vary in their requirements, from a simple review of material to applications of concepts.

I am grateful to Worth Publishers and to Robert Siegler, Judy DeLoache, and Nancy Eisenberg for the opportunity to work with them on this endeavor. The textbook authors provided guidance throughout the project and placed a great deal of importance on its quality. I would like to thank my editors, Charles Linsmeier, Andrea Musick, Eve Conte, and Stacey Alexander, for their encouragement and support throughout the project.

I hope students find this Study Guide valuable and are able to use it as an integral part of their study and review plan. I welcome any suggestions for improvement.

JLS

CHAPTER 1
An Introduction to Child Development

Learning Objectives

Following the completion of the study of Chapter 1, you should be able to:

1. Understand three good reasons for learning about child development.

2. Identify a strength and a limitation in the contributions of philosophers and early scientific theorists to the study of child development.

3. Explain seven enduring themes in child development.

4. Summarize the authors' perspectives on the contemporary positions on each of the seven basic questions about child development. (See In-Class Activity 1.)

5. Describe the procedures involved in the scientific method.

6. Name three important criteria for good measurement.

7. Define three contexts for gathering data and summarize the advantages and disadvantages of each.

8. Recognize and label examples of correlational designs.

9. Identify the risks and benefits associated with the use of correlational designs.

10. Recognize and label the essential components of experimental designs, including random assignment, experimental and control groups, independent variables, and dependent variables.

11. Explain the major advantage and disadvantage of experimental designs. Describe a technique for overcoming the major limitation of experimental designs.

12. Recognize and label examples of each of the three designs for studying development.

13. Name several ethical responsibilities of researchers.

You Should Know:

Introduction

- how Werner's Kauai study was unique and what it demonstrated about the influence of biological and environmental factors.

Why Study Child Development? (*summary on pg. 7 of text*)

Raising Children
- how child-development research can inform parents and teachers.

Choosing Social Policies
- how child-development research can inform social policy.
- how child-development research led to a different understanding of the factors involved in children's testimonies in legal settings.

Understanding Human Nature
- how child-development research can help us better understand human nature in general.
- what research on Romanian orphans has demonstrated about the importance of early experience and the relevance of the timing of experiences.

Historical Foundations of the Study of Child Development
(*summary on pg.10 of text*)

Early Philosophical Views of Children's Development
- what Plato, Aristotle, Locke, and Rousseau thought about children, whether they possessed innate knowledge, and how they should be disciplined, as well as on what these views were based.

The Beginnings of Research on Children
- what sparked the research-based approach to understanding child development.
- how Freud's and Watson's theories were an improvement, still with limitations, over those of their predecessors.

Enduring Themes in Child Development (*summary on pg. 23 of text*)

1. Nature and Nurture

- what is meant by nature and what is meant by nurture.
- what types of questions researchers generally ask about the influences of nature and nurture.
- how research on low-birth-weight infants has demonstrated the influences of both nature and nurture.

2. The Active Child

- what is meant by "the active child" and the general ways children influence their own development.
- how children's contribution to their own development changes with age.

3. Continuity/Discontinuity

- what is meant by continuous development and discontinuous development and what stage theories are.
- how the continuity of development can differ depending on one's perspective.

4. Mechanisms of Developmental Change

- how the evolutionary perspective has provided a useful framework for thinking about how change occurs.

5. The Sociocultural Context

- what is meant by the sociocultural context and what methods researchers generally use to examine the impact of the sociocultural context.
- what this research has demonstrated about the effect of family sleeping arrangements on children.
- how the sociocultural context can vary within a particular culture and across cultures.

6. Individual Differences

- the sources of individual differences, especially among members of the same family.

7. Research and Children's Welfare

- how an understanding of child development can lead to practical benefits for children.
- how this understanding has led to benefits for children in the visual and learning domains.

Methods for Studying Child Development (*summary on pg. 37 of text*)

The Scientific Method

- the basic assumption and steps of the scientific method and how this differs from prior methods.
- the key properties of good scientific measures.

Contexts for Gathering Data About Children

- the three main contexts for gathering information about children, as well as examples of research using these contexts.
- what each context offers researchers in terms of the information they can collect, as well as the disadvantages of each context.

Correlation and Causation

- the goals of studies using correlational designs and experimental designs.
- what a correlation is and the characteristics of the correlation coefficient.
- what a correlation can tell you and what it cannot tell you.
- the logic behind experimental designs and random assignments.
- the types of groups and variables in an experimental design.
- the advantages and disadvantages of experimental designs and how naturalistic experiments overcome some of these limitations.

Designs for Examining Development

- the characteristics of cross-sectional, longitudinal, and microgenetic designs, with examples of each.
- the goals and advantages of these three designs, as well as their limitations.

Ethical Issues in Child-Development Research

- the important aspects of the ethical code for research with children.

Key Term Matching I: Definitions

Instructions: Match each key term with its definition.

Set A

KEY TERM

1. _____ hypotheses

2. _____ correlation

3. _____ dependent variable

4. _____ interrater reliability

5. _____ correlation coefficient

6. _____ variation

7. _____ variables

8. _____ control group

9. _____ third-variable problem

10. _____ direction-of-causation problem

11. _____ independent variable

12. _____ internal validity

13. _____ experimental group

14. _____ nature

15. _____ selection

16. _____ nurture

17. _____ test-retest reliability

18. _____ scientific method

19. _____ external validity

DEFINITION

a. the degree to which the results of research can be generalized beyond the particular children and methods used in the study

b. the experience children in the experimental group receive and children in the control group do not receive

c. the environments, both physical and social, that influence development

d. the more frequent survival and reproduction of organisms that are well-adapted to their environment

e. an approach to testing beliefs that involves choosing a question, formulating a hypothesis, testing the hypothesis, and drawing a conclusion

f. a statistic that indicates the direction and strength of the association between two variables

g. the degree to which different observers of the same behavior agree

h. the degree to which children's performance on two or more occasions is similar

i.   the degree to which the effects observed in experiments can be attributed to the variables that the researcher intentionally manipulated

j.   one's biological endowment; in particular, the genes received from one's parents

k.   attributes that vary across individuals and situations

l.   the association between two variables

m.   educated guesses

n.   the notion that correlations do not indicate which variable, if either, is the cause of the other

o.   the notion that a correlation between two variables could result from both variables being influenced by another, unspecified variable

p.   a group of children in an experimental design that is presented with the experience that is of interest to the researcher

q.   the group of children in an experimental design given an experience identical to that of children in the experimental group, except that they are not presented with the experience of interest to the researcher

r.   differences within and among individuals

s.   a behavior that is hypothesized to be affected by the experience of interest to the researcher

Set B

KEY TERM

20. _____ validity
21. _____ naturalistic experiments
22. _____ clinical interview
23. _____ discontinuous development
24. _____ correlational designs
25. _____ structured interview
26. _____ microgenetic design
27. _____ stage theories
28. _____ longitudinal design
29. _____ experimental designs

30. _____ naturalistic observation
31. _____ experimental control
32. _____ cross-sectional design
33. _____ continuous development
34. _____ structured observation
35. _____ reliability
36. _____ socioeconomic status
37. _____ random assignment
38. _____ sociocultural context

DEFINITION

t. approaches to development that propose development occurs in a series of distinct age-related steps

u. the notion that changes with age occur in sudden, large shifts

v. a method of study in which the same children are studied repeatedly over a short period of time

w. a procedure in which the questions are modified according to participants' responses

x. a measure of social class based on education and income

y. the degree to which independent measurements of a behavior are consistent

z. the degree to which a test measures what it intends to measure

aa. a research method in which all participants are asked the same questions

bb. the notion that changes with age occur gradually

cc. examination of children's behaviors in their usual environments

dd. examination of children's behaviors in an environment where all participants are presented with identical situations

ee. the physical, social, cultural, economic, and historical circumstances that make up a child's environment ff.   studies that allow researchers to make inferences about causes and effects

gg.   a procedure that gives each participant an equal chance of being selected for each group within an experiment

hh.   the ability of the researcher to determine the specific experiences that children in each group encounter during the study

ii.   a type of experimental design in which data are collected in everyday settings rather than in a laboratory

jj.   a research method in which children of different ages are compared on a particular behavior or characteristic

kk.   a research method in which the same children are studied two or more times over a substantial period of time

ll.   studies designed to indicate how variables are related to each other

Key Term Matching II: Applications, Examples, and More

Instructions: Match each key term with an application or example of the term.

Set A

KEY TERM

1.	_____	test-retest reliability	10.	_____	scientific method
2.	_____	selection	11.	_____	hypotheses
3.	_____	interrater reliability	12.	_____	experimental group
4.	_____	dependent variable	13.	_____	nurture
5.	_____	nature	14.	_____	correlation coefficient
6.	_____	internal validity	15.	_____	external validity
7.	_____	third-variable problem	16.	_____	variables
8.	_____	control group	17.	_____	variation
9.	_____	independent variable	18.	_____	direction-of-causation problem

APPLICATION OR EXAMPLE

a.   what differentiates this from past approaches is research methods yield higher-quality evidence allowing for more solid conclusions

b.   examples of these are socioeconomic status, marital status, IQ, and number of friends

c.   the variety of strategies or behaviors an individual has for a particular task is considered

d.   this process involves choosing from among a variety of behaviors or strategies the one that allows individuals to meet their goals consistently, quickly, and easily

e.   although one can control one's environment to some extent, one has no control over the influence of this on development

f.   if both marital conflict and sibling conflict are caused by a family's poor economic circumstances, then a correlation between the two types of conflict would have this

g.   a measure of children's school achievement would be considered to have poor _____ if two teachers demonstrated low levels of agreement on the measure

h.   a measure of children's school achievement would be considered to have high _____ if children who do well on it at one point in time also do well on it later and children who do poorly at one point in time also do poorly on it later

i. if a researcher provides social skills training to children entering first grade and then observes that they have more friends after the training than before, the mere passage of time may be an explanation for a lack of this

j. finding the same results in multiple studies, conducted with different children in different schools and socioeconomic classes and using a variety of methods, establishes the _____ of the findings

k. the prenatal environment (e.g., poor oxygen in the womb as a result of maternal smoking) is considered to be part of this type of influence

l. when this number is high and negative, as in minus .67, it means the knowledge that an individual's score is high on one variable will suggest that his or her score will be low on the other variable

m. a person who concludes a strong correlation between marital conflict and sibling conflict indicates that marital conflict causes sibling conflict, when it could be vice-versa, is demonstrating this

n. these might include, "Children who have a greater number of classmates will develop better social skills" for the research question, "How does the number of children in a classroom relate to children's social skills?"

o. in a study of the effects of social skills training on friendship formation, the children who receive such training comprise this

p. in a study about the effects of social skills training on friendship formation, the children who do not receive the training, but are treated identically otherwise, are in this

q. in a study about the effects of social skills training on friendship formation, the training is referred to as this

r. in a study about the effects of social skills training on friendship formation, the number of friends formed following the training is referred to as this

Set B

KEY TERM

19. _____ discontinuous development   27. _____ correlational designs

20. _____ longitudinal design   28. _____ validity

21. _____ structured observation   29. _____ microgenetic design

22. _____ clinical interview   30. _____ reliability

23. _____ cross-sectional design   31. _____ stage theories

24. _____ experimental designs   32. _____ random assignment

25. _____ continuous development   33. _____ naturalistic observation

26. _____ structured interview   34. _____ naturalistic experiments

APPLICATION OR EXAMPLE

s.   a study in which researchers examine the change in level of sibling conflict after some sibling pairs are taught strategies to decrease conflict while other sibling pairs receive no training is using one of these

t.   a study in which children are asked a series of 10 prepared questions about their sibling relationships is using this method

u.   this method is specifically designed to provide an in-depth depiction of the processes that involve change

v.   this criterion for a good measure could also be referred to as consistency

w.   these still employ random assignment, but have greater external validity than laboratory experiments do

x.   stage theories support the idea of this type of development

y.   a study in which children are probed as to their feelings about their siblings by a researcher who deviates from the script to adjust to particular children's responses is using this method

z.   a study in which children's sibling relationships are examined by mounting unobtrusive cameras throughout their home is using this method

aa. a study in which children's sibling relationships are examined by bringing sibling pairs into the laboratory and asking them to complete a series of puzzles is using this method

bb. a study in which the researcher examines the association between marital conflict and sibling rivalry is using one of these cc.   a focus on the large differences between children of different ages, such as the difference between a nonverbal infant and a preschooler who speaks in complete sentences, may lead to a view that is in *opposition* to the idea of this type of development

dd.   the logic behind this procedure is that groups created in this manner should be comparable on any variable at the beginning of the experiment

ee.   this criterion for a good measure of marital conflict would not be met if children are asked to rate the degree of conflict between their parents as some parents score low simply because they argue only behind closed doors

ff.   a study in which children who are two-, four-, six-, and eight-year-olds are simultaneously compared on the number of words in their vocabulary is utilizing this

gg.   a study in which children are followed from the age of two to eight and the number of words in their vocabulary is examined every two years is utilizing this

hh.   Piaget's theory of cognitive development, Freud's theory of psychosexual development, and Kohlberg's theory of moral development are all these

True/False Questions

Instructions: Indicate whether each item is true or false.

_____	1. One way to ensure accurate testimony from children is to utilize the turtle technique.
_____	2. Children who were adopted after the age of six months from Romanian orphanages into British families generally demonstrated negative consequences in physical, social, and intellectual development.
_____	3. "Nature" includes the physical nature of the womb.
_____	4. Mothers' behavior toward their low-birth-weight infants is unlikely to help prevent later cognitive problems.
_____	5. Children's attentional patterns are one way in which they influence their own development.
_____	6. Teenagers are less likely to influence their own development than are younger children, because parents of teenagers actively attempt to "reel in" their teenagers.
_____	7. During brain development, selection of synapses from the tremendous amount of variation in the brain involves including those synapses that are used and eliminating those synapses that are not used.
_____	8. Sociocultural context can vary from one culture to another, as well as from one historical period to another for the same culture.
_____	9. The four factors that Scarr identified as relevant to individual differences apply *only* to individuals from different families.
_____	10. One reason children may react differently to the same event is that their subjective interpretations of the event may vary.
_____	11. Rarely does child development research lead to practical benefits for real children.
_____	12. Key to the scientific method is the understanding that if many knowledgeable researchers share a belief, it must be correct, and research indicating otherwise must be flawed.
_____	13. The internal validity of an experiment refers to whether the conditions manipulated by the experimenter actually caused the observed effects.
_____	14. The structured interview is useful when the same information is to be collected from all of the people being studied.
_____	15. One limitation of naturalistic observation is that the researcher may not be able to pinpoint exactly which variables in the environment actually influenced the behavior of interest.

_____ 16. The qualities on which individuals differ, such as socioeconomic status, academic ability, and hair color, are referred to as variations.

_____ 17. A correlation coefficient of 1.00 between Characteristic A and Characteristic B indicates that Characteristic A causes Characteristic B.

_____ 18. The group of participants in an experiment that receives the experimental manipulation is referred to as the control group because the experimenter exerts experimental control over this group's experiences.

_____ 19. Longitudinal designs are particularly useful for research questions involving change and stability over time in the same individuals.

_____ 20. Informed consent from parents or other responsible adults must be obtained before conducting research involving children.

Multiple-Choice Questions

1. Werner's Kauai study demonstrated which of the following?
   A. Some biological disadvantages lead to long-term negative outcomes only if there are also environmental disadvantages.
   B. Biological disadvantages cannot be overcome by environmental advantages.
   C. Environmental disadvantages cannot be overcome by biological advantages.
   D. Biological disadvantages can always be overcome by environmental advantages.

2. Which of the following historical figures emphasized the importance of giving children the greatest amount of freedom so that they can learn through their own spontaneous interactions with objects and other people?
   A. Aristotle
   B. Locke
   C. Plato
   D. Rousseau

3. Watson based his theory of child development in large part on which of the following?
   A. hypnosis and analysis of dreams and childhood memories
   B. systematic daily diary of a single child's growth
   C. experiments on reward and punishment of rats and other animals
   D. study of children working in coal mines

4. The finding that children who grow up in troubled homes are more likely than other children to become schizophrenic is evidence of:
   A. the influence of nature.
   B. the influence of nurture.
   C. the interaction of nature and nurture.
   D. random variation in the population.

5. Which of the following pieces of evidence would provide the most support for the influence of nature on the development of empathy?
   A. In comparison with other adopted children, the only children who show high levels of empathy are those whose biological parents are empathetic and who grow up with caring and altruistic parents.
   B. Children who grow up with caring and altruistic parents are more likely than other children to be empathetic, even when adopted as infants.
   C. Children whose biological parents are empathetic are more likely than other children to be empathetic, even when adopted as infants.
   D. There is no association between parents' characteristics and children's empathy.

6. The "active" child refers to which of the following?
   A. children whose environments impact their development
   B. children as shapers of their own development
   C. children who have been diagnosed with attention deficit hyperactivity disorder
   D. children whose biology affects their development

7. Which of the following does not belong with the others?
   A. discontinuous
   B. stage
   C. gradual
   D. qualitatively different

8. Which of the following is NOT generally considered to constitute part of the sociocultural context of a child's life?
   A. the price of milk
   B. child abuse laws
   C. intelligence of child
   D. school teachers' training

9. Children with specific language impairment were assisted by research on:
   A. individual differences.
   B. successive approximation.
   C. preferential looking.
   D. sociocultural context.

10. Which of the following is NOT one of the four steps of the scientific method?
    A. drawing a conclusion
    B. publishing research so parents and educators can benefit from it
    C. developing a method to test the hypothesis
    D. choosing a question

11. Which of the following indicates that a measure of preschoolers' peer acceptance has poor reliability?
    A. Teacher A and Teacher B disagree about which children are liked and which are disliked.
    B. Children's reports of who they like and dislike on one day differ from their reports the following day.
    C. Researchers' counts of how many times a child is asked to play a game are unrelated to how much other children say they like that child.
    D. A and B only
    E. all of the above

12. To examine the effectiveness of empathy training on children's sharing behavior, two months of training is provided to three-year-old children living in rural Georgia. Six months later, the children's sharing behaviors are measured and compared to their pre-training sharing behavior. Improvements are considered the result of the empathy training. Which of the following is a potential source of external invalidity?
A. All children were from rural Georgia.
B. The observers of the sharing behavior may disagree with each other.
C. Children's sharing behavior may improve with the simple passage of time.
D. Children who were the best sharers before the training were not necessarily the best after the training.

13. A clinical interview would probably be the method of choice for a researcher interested in:
A. how young children negotiate with each other when there is only a single desirable toy.
B. the frequency of sexual harassment behavior among adolescents.
C. the extent to which the children in an elementary school class like to play with each other.
D. obtaining extensive information about a single child's feelings about his friendships.

14. Which of the following is a disadvantage of structured observation?
A. Memory of participants for past events is often inaccurate and incomplete.
B. It is difficult to isolate the aspects of the situation that are most influential.
C. Reports are often biased to reflect favorably on the participants.
D. It has a limited value for studying infrequent behaviors.
E. None of the above is a disadvantage of structured observation.

15. Variables X and Y are positively correlated. This correlation indicates which of the following?
A. As the level of X increases, the level of Y decreases.
B. As the level of Y increases, the level of X decreases.
C. As the level of Y increases, the level of X increases.
D. As the level of X decreases, the level of Y decreases.
E. A and B are true.
F. C and D are true.

16. A correlation coefficient of −.80 indicates that, as the level of one variable increases, the level of the other variable:
A. increases.
B. decreases.
C. stays the same.
D. varies randomly.

17. The direction-of-causation problem refers to the fact that:
  A. experimental designs cannot specify cause and effect.
  B. a correlation does not indicate which variable is the cause and which is the effect.
  C. researchers often mistake negative correlations for positive ones.
  D. the correlation between two variables might be caused by an unspecified variable.

18. A class of third-grade children is split into two groups through random assignment. Group A is given training in a new game and Group B is not. Both groups are then tested on their skill in playing the new game. We consider Group A to be the _____ group and Group B to be the _____ group.
  A. dependent; independent
  B. independent; dependent
  C. control; experimental
  D. experimental; control

19. Which of the following could NOT be examined with an experimental design?
  A. effect of physical attractiveness on children's school grades
  B. effect of amount of homework on teenage drinking behavior
  C. effect of TV violence on preschoolers' aggressive behavior
  D. effect of parental discipline practices on children's peer relations

20. A researcher interested in the development of reading skills follows a group of children from age six to age ten. Every six months, children are given a reading test. This researcher is using which type of design?
  A. experimental
  B. microgenetic
  C. longitudinal
  D. cross-sectional

Essay Questions

Instructions: Answer the following essay questions on a separate sheet of paper.

1. Describe the biological and environmental factors you believe may influence the development of walking. In your discussion of this topic, be sure to think about the following questions: Are there any biological factors that you believe may be unaffected by environment (exert their influence regardless of the environment)? Are there any environmental factors that you believe may be unaffected by biology (exert their influence regardless of biology)? In contrast, are there biological factors that may exert an influence only in particular environments? Are there any environmental factors that may exert an influence only when particular biological characteristics are present?

2. Rachel is a six-month-old who has just learned to sit up on her own. Her mother places two toys in front of her, a soft yellow stuffed animal within her reach and a colorful rattle slightly out of her reach. Seeing both toys, Rachel chooses the one she finds more interesting. Over time, Rachel makes many such choices among a variety of objects. From the perspective of children as active participants in their own development, describe three examples of how Rachel's choice of toys to play with may impact her development. You may think about the development of motor skills, likes and dislikes, the understanding of the way different objects function, or any other aspects of development you think may be influenced by choices such as these.

3. Describe how variation and selection might function in the development of the ability to complete puzzles.

4. A researcher is interested in examining sex differences in children's ability to join a group of peers already playing a game. Design two studies to examine this issue, one using structured observation and the other using naturalistic observation. Describe the advantages and disadvantages of each method.

5. Imagine you are a researcher interested in developmental changes in children's strategies for getting others to share. Briefly describe how you could examine this using each of the following designs: (a) cross-sectional, (b) longitudinal, and (c) microgenetic. For each design, be sure to indicate what research question you would be addressing.

Answer Key

Key Term Matching I

1. m	7. k	13. p	19. a	25. aa	31. hh	37. gg
2. l	8. q	14. j	20. z	26. v	32. jj	38. ee
3. s	9. o	15. d	21. ii	27. t	33. bb	
4. g	10. n	16. c	22. w	28. kk	34. dd	
5. f	11. b	17. h	23. u	29. ff	35. y	
6. r	12. i	18. e	24. ll	30. cc	36. x	

Key Term Matching II

1. h	6. i	11. n	16. b	21. aa	26. t	31. hh
2. d	7. f	12. o	17. c	22. y	27. bb	32. dd
3. g	8. p	13. k	18. m	23. ff	28. ee	33. z
4. r	9. q	14. l	19. x	24. s	29. u	34. w
5. e	10. a	15. j	20. gg	25. cc	30. v	

True/False Questions

1. F	6. F	11. F	16. F
2. T	7. T	12. F	17. F
3. F	8. T	13. T	18. F
4. F	9. F	14. T	19. T
5. T	10. T	15. T	20. T

Multiple-Choice Questions

1. A	6. B	11. D	16. B
2. D	7. C	12. A	17. B
3. C	8. C	13. D	18. D
4. B	9. B	14. E	19. A
5. C	10. B	15. F	20. C

CHAPTER 2
Prenatal Development and the Newborn Period

Learning Objectives

Following the completion of the study of Chapter 2, you should be able to:

1. Describe the major structural changes that occur during each of the three major periods of prenatal development: the period of the zygote, the period of the embryo, and the period of the fetus.

2. Apply the principle of **cephalocaudal development** to prenatal development.

3. Give at least two examples of the ways in which the fetus's behavior contributes to its own development.

4. Provide evidence for human fetal learning.

5. Explain how the effects of the environment begin before conception.

6. Name common **teratogens** and explain the factors associated with the likelihood that exposure to teratogens will result in birth defects.

7. Explain the ways in which the process of being born contributes to the postnatal survival of the fetus.

8. Recognize different states of arousal in the newborn.

9. Explain the ways in which the sleep state changes over development.

10. Know what to say to parents who ask how they should respond to the newborn's cries.

11. Name the reasons for the relatively high rate of infant mortality in the United States.

12. Describe the outcomes associated with low birth weight.

13. Understand the **multiple-risk model** as it is applied to the impact of poverty on development.

You Should Know:

Prenatal Development (*summary on pg. 67 of text*)

Introduction
- how modern scientific techniques have changed the view of prenatal development.

Box 2.1: Beng Beginnings
- how cultural beliefs about when life begins can underlie childrearing beliefs and practices.

Conception
- how sperm and egg are formed.
- how conception occurs and what it involves.

Box 2.2: The First Sex Differences
- the differences between males and females in their rates of their conception, miscarriage, and survival, as well as in their vulnerability to developmental disorders.
- how sociocultural context can influence the differential survival of males and females.

Developmental Processes
- the four major developmental processes that underlie the transformation of a zygote into an embryo and then into a fetus.
- how the flexibility of cells changes as they develop.
- the role of hormones in sexual differentiation.

Box 2.3: Phylogenetic Continuity
- the rationale behind analogies made between humans and other animals.

Early Development
- how different types of twins originate.
- the processes by which the zygote transforms into an embryo and the embryo develops.
- the functions of the components of the embryo's support system.

An Illustrated Summary of Prenatal Development
- the general order in which development proceeds.
- the timing of several developmental milestones.

Fetal Behavior
- how the fetus plays an active role in its own physical and behavioral development.
- the types and functions of movements common to the fetus.
- how fetal states are associated with newborn states.
- how behavioral cycles develop.

Fetal Experience
- what the fetus experiences in terms of touch, taste, smell, hearing, and sight.
- how research has demonstrated fetal sensory experience.

Fetal Learning
- what evidence exists for fetuses learning from experiences in the womb.
- how newborn preferences are associated with prenatal experiences.
- what fetuses are probably *unable* to learn.

Hazards to Prenatal Development
- what environmental agents can pose harm to the developing organism and how these agents affect the fetus.
- how the timing and amount of exposure, as well as individual fetal differences, are related to the effect of the agent on the developing organism.
- how maternal factors, such as stress and disease, can influence prenatal development.

Box 2.4: Face Up to Wake Up
- what SIDS is and how it can best be prevented.

The Birth Experience *(summary on pg. 69 of text)*

Introduction
- how the birth process is likely experienced by the baby.
- how the birth process itself serves an adaptive function for the newborn.

Diversity of Childbirth Practices
- how childbirth practices can vary according to cultural values and goals.

The Newborn Infant *(summary on pg. 80 of text)*

State of Arousal
- the pattern and adaptive significance of newborn states and how and why these change with development.

- how infants' state can influence their experience of the world as well as parent-infant interactions.
- how and when caregivers should respond to infant crying.
- the characteristics of colic and how parents can best cope.

Negative Outcomes at Birth

- how and why infant mortality rates differ across countries and across subcultures of the United States.
- the causes and consequences of low birth weight and how intervention programs have been successful and unsuccessful.
- the association between vulnerability and the number of risk factors a baby has.
- how socioeconomic status relates to risk factors.
- the factors associated with developmental resilience.

Box 2.5: Parenting a Low-Birth-Weight Baby

- how and why parenting a low-birth-weight baby is more challenging than parenting normal-weight babies and what parents can do for help.

Key Term Matching I: Definitions

Instructions: Match each key term with its definition.

Set A

KEY TERM

1. _____ amniotic sac

2. _____ fetal alcohol spectrum disorder

3. _____ dose-response relation

4. _____ sleeper effects

5. _____ neural tube

6. _____ low birth weight

7. _____ umbilical cord

8. _____ embryo

9. _____ sudden infant death syndrome (SIDS)

10. _____ premature

11. _____ placenta

12. _____ colic

13. _____ teratogens

14. _____ small for gestational age

15. _____ sensitive period

16. _____ zygote

DEFINITION

a. the unexpected death of an infant that has no identifiable cause

b. the period of time during which a developing organism is most at risk for harm from outside agents

c. babies that weigh substantially less than normal for their gestational age

d. the organ rich with blood vessels that permits the exchange of materials between the bloodstreams of the mother and the fetus

e. the groove formed in the embryo that will eventually develop into its brain and spinal cord

f. a birth weight less than 5.5 lbs.

g. a developing organism in its 3rd to 8th week of prenatal development

h. the fact that the likelihood and severity of a prenatal defect occurring as a result of teratogen exposure is associated with the level of exposure to the teratogen

i. excessive crying occurring in the first few months of life that occurs for no apparent reason

j. the membrane that is filled with a clear, watery fluid in which the fetus floats

k.   the range of effects of prenatal exposure to alcohol

l.   the fertilized egg

m.   the tube that contains the blood vessels running between the mother and the fetus

n.   consequences of teratogens that are not apparent immediately

o.   a child born at or before 35 weeks following conception

p.   environmental agents that can cause harm to the developing organism

Set B

KEY TERM

17. _____ conception

18. _____ swaddling

19. _____ identical twins

20. _____ state

21. _____ phylogenic continuity

22. _____ non-REM sleep

23. _____ habituation

24. _____ developmental resilience

25. _____ cephalocaudal development

26. _____ epigenesis

27. _____ apoptosis

28. _____ fraternal twins

29. _____ autostimulation theory

30. _____ embryology

31. _____ gametes

32. _____ REM

DEFINITION

q.   an infant's level of arousal and engagement in the environment

r.   a form of learning that involves a decrease in response to repeated stimulation

s.   cell death that is programmed

t.   the notion that brain activity during REM sleep facilitates the early development of the visual system in the fetus and newborn

u.   a quiet or deep sleep characterized by the absence of motor activity and eye movements

v.   the union of sperm and egg

w.   an active sleep state characterized by quick, jerky eye movements

x.   the notion that humans share some characteristics and developmental processes with other animals as a result of our common evolutionary history

y.   a soothing technique which involves wrapping an infant tightly in a blanket

z.   siblings that result when the zygote splits in half

aa.   successful development occurring in the face of multiple developmental hazards

bb.   the emergence of new structures and functions during development

cc.   sperm and egg

dd.   the pattern of growth in which areas near the head develop earlier than areas farther away from the head

ee.   the study of prenatal development

ff.   siblings that result when two eggs released into the fallopian tube at the same time are fertilized by two sperm

Key Term Matching II: Applications, Examples, and More

Instructions: Match each key term with an application or example of the term.

Set A

KEY TERM

1. _____ colic

2. _____ neural tube

3. _____ sensitive period

4. _____ low birth weight

5. _____ fetal alcohol spectrum disorder

6. _____ umbilical cord

7. _____ sleeper effects

8. _____ teratogens

9. _____ sudden infant death syndrome (SIDS)

10. _____ small for gestational age

11. _____ zygote

12. _____ placenta

13. _____ premature

14. _____ amniotic sac

15. _____ embryo

16. _____ dose-response relation

APPLICATION OR EXAMPLE

a. symptoms of the most dramatic form of this include facial deformities, mental retardation, and organ defects

b. DES demonstrated these when babies whose mothers had received it demonstrated a higher risk of testicular and cervical cancer in adolescence and adulthood

c. this organ allows oxygen, nutrients, and minerals to pass from the mother to the developing organism, but does not allow their blood to mix

d. a baby born at 34 weeks following conception who weighs 6.5 lbs. is this

e. the amount and length of exposure to potentially harmful environmental agents is crucial in determining the effect of exposure because of this

f. a baby born full-term who weighs less than is normal is considered to be of low birth weight *and* this

g. cell division begins during this period of prenatal development

h. fusion of the U-shaped groove in the top layer of the differentiated inner cell mass forms this

i.   as a result of the existence of this, *only* babies who were exposed to thalidomide while the limbs were emerging and developing were born with major limb deformities

j.   babies with this are more likely to suffer from hearing, language, and cognitive impairments, as well as a variety of social problems

k.   this contains the fluid that cushions the developing organism from jolts

l.   the inner cell mass differentiates into three layers during this period of prenatal development

m.   these include legal and illegal drugs, as well as environmental pollutants such as mercury

n.   the risk of this is decreased by putting babies to sleep on their backs

o.   this tube runs between the placenta and the fetus

p.   this may cause parents to feel inadequate in their ability to soothe their baby

Set B

KEY TERM

17. _____ non-REM sleep

18. _____ fraternal twins

19. _____ phylogenic continuity

20. _____ embryology

21. _____ identical twins

22. _____ autostimulation theory

23. _____ apoptosis

24. _____ epigenesis

25. _____ cephalocaudal development

26. _____ developmental resilience

27. _____ conception

28. _____ state

29. _____ habituation

30. _____ REM

31. _____ gametes

32. _____ swaddling

APPLICATION OR EXAMPLE

q.   support for this was demonstrated by giving newborns extra visual stimulation while they were awake

r.   this is a rejection of the idea of preformation

s.   this may help make up for the little visual stimulation experienced by fetuses and newborns

t.   the result of this is a zygote

u.   this is the study of physical and behavioral development in the womb

v.   this technique restricts the limb movement of the infant

w.   this affects young infants' experience of the world and can range from deep sleep to intense activity

x.   this pattern explains why the hands develop before the feet

y.   twins who share half of their genetic material

z.   this principle enables research on fetal exposure to alcohol conducted with mice to be applicable to humans

aa.   these cells contain only half of the genetic material usually found in a cell

bb.   children who demonstrate this often have a responsive caregiver and personal characteristics such as intelligence and a sense of being capable of achieving their goals cc.   an example of this is the death of cells in between the ridges in the hand plate of the developing organism

dd.   this is one of the simplest forms of learning and was demonstrated when fetuses were repeatedly presented with a recording of the sound "babi"

ee.   individuals with the exact same genetic makeup

ff.   this is characterized by slow brain waves, breathing, and heart rate

True/False Questions

Instructions: Indicate whether each item is true or false.

_____ 1. "Minamata Disease" is an example of how negligence in the care of low-birth-weight babies can have lasting consequences.

_____ 2. Gametes contain half the genetic material found in other cells.

_____ 3. Stem cells are embryonic cells that have migrated to a particular location and have begun to specialize in structure and function.

_____ 4. The placental membrane serves as a perfect barrier against elements that could be harmful to the fetus.

_____ 5. The normal formation of muscles and organs depends on fetal activity.

_____ 6. The sleep states of the fetus in the last two weeks before birth are highly similar to those of the newborn.

_____ 7. Fetuses have no olfactory (smell) experiences because they take no air or fluid through their nose.

_____ 8. Fetuses can hear various sounds during the last trimester, and these noises elicit changes in the movements and heart rate of the fetus.

_____ 9. A group of 37-week-old fetuses whose mothers repeatedly recited a short rhyme over the course of several weeks learned to recognize the rhyme.

_____ 10. In order for an infant to ever prefer the sound of her father's voice over the sound of other men's voices, she must have been exposed to it while in the womb.

_____ 11. Approximately 20% of all pregnancies end in miscarriage.

_____ 12. Nearly all teratogenic damage occurs once women already know they are pregnant, so as long as newly-pregnant women are aware of potentially harmful environmental agents, their babies should be fine.

_____ 13. The most common preventable cause of mental retardation and birth defects in the United States is maternal alcohol use during pregnancy.

_____ 14. In the United States, infants from low-income families are more likely to die from SIDS than are other infants.

_____ 15. Some maternal illness and disease appear to affect the fetus by increasing the likelihood of psychopathology later in life.

_____ 16. When newborns get squeezed through the birth canal during delivery, they experience moderate to severe discomfort, causing the well-known newborn cry.

_____   17.   There is some evidence that newborns may learn while they are sleeping.

_____   18.   Both touch and taste can have soothing effects for crying newborns.

_____   19.   In the United States, there is no association between poverty and birth weight.

_____   20.   In the Infant Health and Development Project (IDHP) aimed at helping low-birth-weight babies, babies who were very small at birth demonstrated lesser long-term gains in IQ than did babies who were heavier at birth.

Multiple-Choice Questions

1. The study of prenatal development is referred to as:
   A. prenatology.
   B. developmental psychology.
   C. embryology.
   D. genetics.

2. The union of sperm and egg is termed:
   A. apoptosis.
   B. conception.
   C. epigenesis.
   D. mating.

3. Which of the following is an example of cell migration?
   A. splitting of the fertilized egg into two equal parts
   B. death of cells in between the ridges on the hand plate
   C. movement of new cells into the outer layer of the brain
   D. specialization of eye cells

4. The study in which cells located in the eye region of a frog embryo were moved to its belly demonstrated which of the following about cells transplanted early versus later in development?
   A. Cells transplanted early became a *normal part* of the belly, but those transplanted later became an *eye* lodged in the belly.
   B. Cells transplanted early became an *eye* lodged in the belly, but those transplanted later became a *normal part* of the belly.
   C. The cells became a *normal part* of the belly no matter whether they were transplanted early or late in development.
   D. The cells became an *eye* lodged in the belly no matter whether they were transplanted early or late in development.

5. Fraternal twins originate when:
   A. an inner cell mass splits in half.
   B. an embryo splits in half.
   C. two eggs are fertilized by two sperm.
   D. an egg splits and is fertilized by two sperm.

6. Which of the following is NOT part of the fetus' support system?
    A. umbilical cord
    B. amniotic sac
    C. placenta
    D. neural tube

7. What causes fetal hiccups?
    A. The fetus swallows air.
    B. The mother's hiccups are transmitted across the placenta.
    C. The fetus' grasping of the umbilical cord restricts airflow to the fetus.
    D. The cause is unknown.

8. A fetus' activity level while in the uterus is _____ over time, and/but it is _____ to postnatal activity level.
    A. consistent; unrelated
    B. consistent; related
    C. inconsistent; unrelated
    D. inconsistent; related

9. Which of the following is a true statement about fetus' auditory (hearing) experiences during the last few months of the pregnancy?
    A. The fetus' auditory organs are so underdeveloped before birth that it does not have the ability to hear.
    B. The fetus' auditory organs are sufficiently developed to hear, but the amniotic fluid muffles all noises so drastically that the fetus cannot hear anything.
    C. The fetus' auditory organs are sufficiently developed to hear, and the fetus can hear many, but not all, features of internal and external sounds.
    D. The fetus' auditory organs are sufficiently developed to hear, and thus the fetus can hear internal and external noises almost perfectly.

10. Which of the following is evidence that a fetus has habituated to a repeated stimulus?
    A. decreased changes in heart rate
    B. turning towards a stimulus
    C. increased changes in heart rate
    D. increased movement

11. Rhonda is pregnant with twins, Fetus A and Fetus B. She is caught in traffic, and there are car horns blaring every few moments. Both fetuses initially experience a heart rate deceleration. As the car horn blaring continues, however, both fetuses' heart rate response decreases. After several minutes, a church bell rings loudly. The heart rate of Fetus A changes, but the heart rate of Fetus B does not change. Which of the following is NOT a possible explanation for the differences in the responses of the twin fetuses?
    A. Fetus A heard the church bell, whereas Fetus B did not.
    B. Fetus A learned to recognize the sound of the horns, whereas Fetus B did not.
    C. Fetus A recognized the difference between the sounds of the car horns and the church bell, whereas Fetus B did not.
    D. All of the above are possible explanations.

12. Which of the following is NOT a true statement about newborn preferences?
    A. Newborns prefer to listen to their mother's voice over another woman's voice.
    B. Newborns prefer to smell their own amniotic fluid over another baby's amniotic fluid.
    C. Newborns prefer to taste foods their mother ate while they were in the womb over other foods.
    D. Newborns prefer to hear novel sound patterns, such as poems and songs, over sound patterns they heard in the womb.

13. The sensitive period of the majority of major organ systems occurs in which period of prenatal development?
    A. embryonic
    B. fetal
    C. zygotic
    D. The sensitive period is dispersed throughout the entire prenatal period.

14. Which of the following has negative effects on prenatal development?
    A. cigarette smoke
    B. alcohol
    C. cocaine
    D. all of the above

15. Fiona is stressed and depressed during her pregnancy. For which of the following is her baby at greater risk than if Fiona were not stressed or depressed?
    A. high birth weight
    B. behavioral and emotional problems
    C. high-pitched crying
    D. rubella

16. Most newborn infants spend the majority of their day in which of the following states?
   A. autostimulation
   B. sleep
   C. crying
   D. awake alert

17. Which of the following is the *best* explanation for the large amount of time newborns spend in REM sleep?
   A. Newborns just sleep a lot overall.
   B. The brain activity generated during REM sleep partially compensates for the relatively little visual stimulation newborns receive throughout the day.
   C. Newborns have immature nervous systems and thus they are less capable of transitioning from REM to non-REM sleep.
   D. The neurotransmitter production accomplished during REM sleep prompts newborns to cry when they need food.

18. Wrapping a baby tightly in clothes or a blanket is referred to as:
   A. swaddling.
   B. swanking.
   C. swapping.
   D. squeezing.

19. In the poor areas of the city in northeast Brazil that were described in the text where the infant mortality rate is as high as 90%, the infants who are most likely to survive may be those who:
   A. are extremely fatigued and sleep a lot.
   B. are patient and quiet.
   C. cry a lot.
   D. display evidence of malnutrition.

20. A multiple-risk model of prenatal and later development states that multiple risks are likely to:
   A. be cumulative.
   B. counteract each other.
   C. encourage resiliency.
   D. both B and C.

Essay Questions

Instructions: Answer the following essay questions on a separate sheet of paper.

1. Describe the following components of the fetal support system: placenta, umbilical cord, and amniotic sac. For each component, explain what it is as well as what its functions are.

2. Design a study to examine whether 35-week-old fetuses can differentiate between high-pitched melodies and low-pitched melodies. Be specific as to your methodology and what results you would expect if fetuses were able to differentiate between the melodies of different pitches. Then, describe how you could also examine whether the fetuses remembered the melodies over the course of a week. What would the results look like if fetuses were able to remember the melodies?

3. Describe three examples of newborn preferences that are based on prenatal experience.

4. Describe how cultural beliefs and practices can influence the child birth process and treatment of the newborn.

5. Describe what it means when psychologists say that infant crying has adaptive significance.

Answer Key

Key Term Matching I

1. j	6. f	11. d	16. l	21. x	26. bb	31. cc
2. k	7. m	12. i	17. v	22. u	27. s	32. w
3. h	8. g	13. p	18. y	23. r	28. ff	
4. n	9. a	14. c	19. z	24. aa	29. t	
5. e	10. o	15. b	20. q	25. dd	30. ee	

Key Term Matching II

1. p	6. o	11. g	16. e	21. ee	26. bb	31. aa
2. h	7. b	12. c	17. ff	22. q	27. t	32. v
3. i	8. m	13. d	18. y	23. cc	28. w	
4. j	9. n	14. k	19. z	24. r	29. dd	
5. a	10. f	15. l	20. u	25. x	30. s	

True/False Questions

1. F	6. T	11. F	16. F
2. T	7. F	12. F	17. T
3. F	8. T	13. T	18. T
4. F	9. T	14. T	19. F
5. T	10. F	15. T	20. T

Multiple-Choice Questions

1. C	6. D	11. B	16. B
2. B	7. D	12. D	17. B
3. C	8. B	13. A	18. A
4. A	9. C	14. D	19. C
5. C	10. A	15. B	20. A

CHAPTER 3
Biology and Behavior

Learning Objectives

Following the completion of the study of Chapter 3, you should be able to:

1. Identify several mechanisms that contribute to genetic variability.

2. Explain the contribution of the child's genotype to his or her own **phenotype**.

3. Apply the concept of **norm of reaction** to the understanding of the contribution of the child's environment to his or her phenotype.

4. Give an example of the influence of the child's phenotype on the environment.

5. Name the basic research designs used to study **heritability**.

6. Explain the limitations of heritability estimates.

7. Identify the parts of the neuron and the major lobes of the cortex.

8. Explain the developmental processes that bring the human brain into being: **neurogenesis, myelination, synaptogenesis,** and **synapse elimination**.

9. Distinguish between **experience-expectant** and **experience-dependent** processes.

10. Discuss the relationships among **sensitive periods, plasticity, and vulnerability**.

11. Give an example of a **secular trend** in development.

12. Explain the origins of obesity.

13. Understand the ways in which malnutrition interacts with other forms of deprivation and affects all aspects of development.

You Should Know:

Nature and Nurture (*summary on pg. 100 of text*)

Introduction
- how the understanding of the role of nature and nurture has advanced to the present.

- what researchers have learned from decoding the genetic code of humans and other organisms.

Genetic and Environmental Forces

- how the genotype of the parent, the phenotype of the parent, the genotype of the child, the phenotype of the child, and the child's environment are interrelated in a model of genetic and environmental influences on development.

- the process through which the parent's genotype influences the child's genotype, including an understanding of DNA and genetic transmission of genes, sex determination, and why children do not have the same genetic make-up as their parents.

- how the genes of an individual are related to the individual's phenotype, including what determines whether a particular gene is expressed or not and the mechanisms of Mendelian patterns of inheritance and polygenic inheritance.

- how the concepts of a norm of reaction and genotype-environment interactions relate to the association between a child's environment and the child's phenotype.

- how the active child theme comes into play in the association between the child's phenotype and the child's environment.

Box 3.1 Applications: Genetic Transmission of Diseases and Disorders

- the various types of genetically-transmitted diseases and disorders and the ways in which they are genetically transmitted.

Behavior Genetics

- what the field of behavior genetics attempts to decipher, as well as what behavior geneticists presume about all behavioral traits.

- how behavior geneticists examine the proportionate roles of environment and genetics and what premises underlie their research designs.

- how family studies of intelligence have shed light on the contributions of genetics and environment to intelligence.

- what heritability estimates do and do not tell us.

- the sources of shared and nonshared environmental effects and how they are assessed.

Box 3.2 Theory in Action: Identical Twins Reared Apart

- what studies of identical twins reared apart have demonstrated about the heritability of many characteristics, as well as what the potential problems with these studies are.

Brain Development (*summary on pg. 115 of text*)

Structures of the Brain

- what the components of neurons are and what their functions are.
- what the cerebral cortex is, how it is structured, and the general functions of its lobes.
- what the cerebral hemispheres are, how they communicate, and how their modes of processing generally differ.

Developmental Processes

- how the developmental processes of neurogenesis, synaptogenesis, and synapse elimination work to structure the brain prenatally and throughout the lifespan.
- why studying the adolescent brain may provide information about adolescent behavior.
- how nature and nurture influence these developmental processes.

Box 3.3 A Closer Look: Mapping the Mind

- how researchers have employed various techniques to investigate which areas of the brain are associated with particular tasks.

The Importance of Experience

- the mechanism behind the influence of experience on synaptic preservation and elimination.
- why the brain produces an overabundance of synapses.
- how the brain is sculpted through experience-expectant processes, and how this type of plasticity leaves the brain vulnerable (*hint*: sensitive periods).
- how the brain is sculpted through experience-dependent processes.

Brain Damage and Recovery

- how plasticity and timing play roles in recovery from brain damage (i.e., when are the "best" and "worst" times to suffer brain damage?).

The Body: Physical Growth and Development (*summary on pg. 123 of text*)

Growth and Maturation

- the pattern of growth for humans and how growth patterns differ for males and females.
- how secular trends and environmental factors play a role in growth.

Nutritional Behavior

- the benefits of breastfeeding infants and why formula-feeding can support normal growth in some environments but not in others.

- the taste preferences that are present at birth and how experience and parental behavior are associated with taste preferences and eating behavior throughout childhood.
- the causes and consequences of obesity.

Box 3.4 Applications: Eat Your Peas, Please

- what parents should and should not do to encourage healthy eating habits in their children.

Undernutrition

- the types of malnutrition that are problematic in developing nations.
- how malnutrition and poverty interact to affect development and cognitive abilities, including both direct and indirect effects of malnutrition.

Key Term Matching I: Definitions

Instructions: Match each key term with its definition.

Set A

KEY TERM

1. _____ genotype

2. _____ multifactorial

3. _____ environment

4. _____ phenotype

5. _____ alleles

6. _____ experience-expectant plasticity

7. _____ norm of reaction

8. _____ cerebral cortex

9. _____ experience-dependent plasticity

10. _____ heritability

11. _____ heritable

12. _____ lobes

13. _____ cerebral hemispheres

14. _____ corpus callosum

15. _____ polygenic inheritance

16. _____ genes

17. _____ genome

DEFINITION

a. the two halves of the cortex

b. the concept that refers to all of the possible phenotypes that could result from a particular genotype in relation to all possible environments

c. the observable expression of the inherited genetic material, including physical and behavioral characteristics

d. a dense band of nerve fibers that allows communication between the two cerebral hemispheres

e. the basic units of heredity

f. inheritance in which several different genes contribute to a particular trait

g. the genetic material inherited by an individual

h. traits or characteristics influenced by genetic factors

i. the involvement of many factors, such as genetic and environmental factors, in an outcome

j.   the process by which neural connections are created and reorganized as a result of an individual's idiosyncratic experiences

k.   the gray matter of the brain

l.   a statistical estimate of the proportion of variability across individuals that is due to genetic differences among those individuals

m.   the complete set of genes possessed by an organism

n.   all aspects of the individual and his or her surroundings other than the genes themselves

o.   the process by which the normal wiring of the brain occurs as a result of the general experiences that every human in a reasonably normal environment will have

p.   major areas of the cortex

q.   different forms of a gene for a particular trait

Set B

KEY TERM

18. _____ axons
19. _____ crossing over
20. _____ regulator genes
21. _____ recessive allele
22. _____ myelination
23. _____ glial cells
24. _____ dendrites
25. _____ mutation

26. _____ synapses
27. _____ cell body
28. _____ myelin sheath
29. _____ neurons
30. _____ synaptogenesis
31. _____ neurogenesis
32. _____ secular trends
33. _____ dominant allele

DEFINITION

r. a change in a section of DNA

s. the process by which neurons form connections with other neurons

t. neural fibers that conduct electrical impulses away from the cell body toward connections with other cells

u. the allele that, if present, gets expressed

v. genes that control the activity of other genes, such as switching on and off

w. cells that are specialized for sending and receiving electrical messages within the brain and between the brain and all parts of the body

x. the part of the neuron that contains the biological material that keeps the cell functioning

y. discernible changes in physical development that have occurred over generations

z. the production of neurons through cell division

aa. cells in the brain that provide supportive functions

bb. the junctions between the axons of one cell and the dendrites of another

cc. the formation of the fatty insulation around some axons

dd. the process by which two members of a pair of chromosomes swap sections of DNA

ee. the allele that is *not* expressed if a dominant allele is present

ff. neural fibers that receive input from other cells and direct it toward the cell body gg. the fatty insulation around some axons that increases speed and efficiency of information transmission in the nervous system

Set C

KEY TERM

34. _____ phenylketonuria

35. _____ plasticity

36. _____ parietal lobe

37. _____ homozygous

38. _____ heterozygous

39. _____ chromosomes

40. _____ behavior genetics

41. _____ marasmus

42. _____ temporal lobe

43. _____ sex chromosomes

44. _____ frontal lobe

45. _____ failure-to-thrive

46. _____ cerebral lateralization

47. _____ spines

48. _____ DNA

49. _____ association areas

50. _____ occipital lobe

51. _____ kwashiorkor

DEFINITION

hh.   long, threadlike molecules made up of two twisted strands of genetic material

ii.   molecules that carry the biochemical instructions involved in the formation and functioning of an organism

jj.   the chromosomes that determine an individual's gender

kk.   the lobe of the brain that is associated with memory and visual recognition, as well as the processing of emotional and auditory information

ll.   the phenomenon that each half of the brain is specialized for different modes of processing

mm.   a disorder related to a recessive gene that can cause severe mental retardation if the affected individual is not prevented from eating foods containing the amino acid phenylalanine

nn.   malnutrition brought about by the intake of inadequate protein

oo.   the lobe of the brain that is primarily involved in processing visual information

pp.   when a person has two of the same allele for a particular trait

qq.   the lobe of the brain that governs spatial processing and integration of sensory input with information stored in memory

rr.   formations on dendrites that increase the dendrites' capacity to form connections with other neurons ss.   parts of the brain that lie between major sensory and motor areas and that process and integrate input from those areas

tt.   when a person has two different alleles for a particular trait

uu.   the lobe of the brain that is associated with organizing behavior and planning ahead

vv.   the capacity of the brain to be affected by experience

ww.   a condition in which infants become malnourished and do not grow for no obvious medical reason

xx.   malnutrition brought about by the intake of too few calories

yy.   the area of psychology concerned with how variation in behavior results from a combination of genetic and environmental factors

Key Term Matching II: Applications, Examples, and More

Instructions: Match each key term with an application or example of the term.

Set A

KEY TERM

1. _____ norm of reaction

2. _____ cerebral hemispheres

3. _____ failure-to-thrive

4. _____ environment

5. _____ cerebral lateralization

6. _____ dominant allele

7. _____ recessive allele

8. _____ polygenic inheritance

9. _____ experience-dependent plasticity

10. _____ behavior genetics

11. _____ genome

12. _____ genotype

13. _____ genes

14. _____ phenotype

15. _____ cerebral cortex

16. _____ secular trends

17. _____ experience-expectant plasticity

APPLICATION OR EXAMPLE

a. mapping of the human _____ has demonstrated how much we have in common with other species

b. because the allele for brown hair is this, a child with brown hair must have at least one parent who has brown hair

c. this is a result of environmental factors acting in concert with genetic makeup

d. scientists in this field believe that *all* behavioral traits are heritable and that all develop within an environment

e. each of these codes for the production of a particular protein

f. most psychological and behavioral traits involve this, rather than Mendelian patterns

g. an example of this is the fact that American girls of today are experiencing menarche at an earlier age than did their ancestors

h. an individual's inheritance of two "brown hair" genes is considered to be part of this

i.   this concept could be demonstrated by cloning an individual numerous times, placing the clones in a variety of environments, and observing differences in a trait such as intelligence or height

j.   identical twins differ in observable characteristics because of differences in this

k.   because the allele for blond hair is this, a child with blond hair may have parents who both have brown hair

l.   in general, these receive sensory information from and control the motor functions of the opposite side of the body

m.   an individual who generally appears to process information in a piecemeal, logical manner may be called "left-brained" by his friends because of this phenomenon

n.   this is considered to be the most human part of the brain, and it constitutes 80% of the human brain

o.   as a result of this type of plasticity, individuals are able to remember new faces and names

p.   this appears to be associated with disturbances in the mother-child interaction that occur as a result of characteristics of both the mother and the child

q.   as a result of this type of plasticity, individuals born with a lazy eye who do not receive treatment can become blind, as the affected eye is essentially disconnected from the brain

Set B

KEY TERM

18.	_____	alleles	27. _____	heritability
19.	_____	synaptogenesis	28. _____	neurons
20.	_____	sex chromosomes	29. _____	puberty
21.	_____	plasticity	30. _____	heterozygous
22.	_____	crossing over	31. _____	neurogenesis
23.	_____	chromosomes	32. _____	DNA
24.	_____	homozygous	33. _____	mutation
25.	_____	glial cells	34. _____	synapses
26.	_____	phenylketonuria		

APPLICATION OR EXAMPLE

r.   humans have 23 pairs of these

s.   different sequences of this are associated with different traits

t.   dendrites and axons are components of these

u.   many inherited diseases and disorders originate from this mechanism for genetic diversity

v.   an individual who is _____ for a trait will definitely express this allele, whether it is dominant or recessive

w.   the gene for brown hair and the gene for blond hair are these

x.   as a result of this mechanism for genetic diversity, the chromosomes that parents pass on to their offspring are different from their own

y.   an individual who has one gene for blue eyes and one for brown eyes is considered this

z.   this developmental process is essentially complete by approximately 18 weeks following conception

aa.   the strengthening of some synapses and the elimination of others that occurs as a result of experience is a demonstration of this brain capacity

bb.   a female has two of the same; a male has two different _____

cc.   neurons' electrical impulses are translated into chemical messages in these

dd.   these work to form a myelin sheath around some axons

ee. the potential effect of this inherited disorder on affected individuals is a great example of a genotype-environmental interaction

ff. this developmental process begins prenatally and proceeds for some time after birth and results in a huge surplus of connections among neurons

gg. estimates of this tell us nothing about the contribution of genetic factors to the characteristics of a particular individual

hh. this developmental stage can lead to negative attitudes toward one's body, especially for girls

True/False Questions

Instructions: Indicate whether each item is true or false.

_____ 1. The mapping of the human genome has resulted in the conclusion that humans have approximately 100,000 genes, and a surprisingly small proportion of these are common to animals outside of the mammal class.

_____ 2. The observable expression of the inherited genetic material is referred to as an individual's phenotype.

_____ 3. It is the presence of only one X chromosome that makes an individual a male.

_____ 4. During meiosis, the pairs of chromosomes are shuffled randomly, and thus chance determines which member of each pair will go into each new sperm or egg.

_____ 5. The same gene can have both beneficial and harmful effects.

_____ 6. Regulator genes are responsible for many gene-induced events associated with aging.

_____ 7. The norm of reaction refers to all of the possible genotypes that could theoretically result from two particular parents.

_____ 8. Parents' behavior toward their children and the environment that they create for their children is due in part to the parents' own genetic makeup.

_____ 9. The model of the associations among parents' and children's genotypes, parents' and children's phenotypes, and the environment discussed in the text does *not* account for the active child theme.

_____ 10. Behavior geneticists use family studies, comparing the correlations among individuals who vary in the extent of their genetic relatedness, to assess the extent to which genetics play a part in a particular trait or behavior.

_____ 11. Behavior geneticists assume that the degree of similarity of the environment is the same for identical twins who grow up together and fraternal twins who grow up together.

_____ 12. As fraternal twins get older, their increasing control over their own environments leads to their increasingly similar IQs.

_____ 13. A high heritability estimate indicates that a substantial amount of the variation in a particular trait among individuals in a particular group is due to differences in their genes.

_____ 14. The finding that the risk of schizophrenia is the same for the biological child of a schizophrenic parent regardless of whether the child is raised by that parent or is adopted away at birth is evidence of the importance of the shared environment.

_____   15.   It has become increasingly clear that complex mental functions are performed independently by single areas of the brain.

_____   16.   Sensitive periods are a particularly important element of experience-expectant plasticity.

_____   17.   The language functions of young children shift to intact areas of the brain following brain damage to the language area of the cortex, but this reorganization does not occur in adults who suffer similar damage.

_____   18.   Higher levels of obesity among children today have resulted in a secular trend – girls today begin menstruating a year or two later than their ancestors did.

_____   19.   Preschoolers are quite poor at regulating the amount of food they consume, and thus parents must control their eating habits.

_____   20.   The weight of adopted children is more strongly correlated with the weight of their adoptive parents than it is with the weight of their biological parents.

Multiple-Choice Questions

1. The genetic material an individual inherits is referred to as the individual's:
    A. genome.
    B. genotype.
    C. phenotype.
    D. environment.

2. Which of the following is a mechanism for genetic differences between parents and offspring?
    A. crossing over
    B. mutation
    C. random assortment in the formation of germ cells
    D. All of the above are mechanisms for genetic differences between parents and offspring.

3. Traits that involve polygenic inheritance:
    A. are more likely to be expressed in males.
    B. are exhibited only when an individual is heterozygous for the trait.
    C. are produced from a combination of multiple genes.
    D. follow the Mendelian pattern of inheritance.

4. Disease Z is a dominant-gene disease. Individuals with which of the following genetic patterns will suffer from Disease Z?
    A. those with one Disease Z gene and one healthy gene
    B. those with two Disease Z genes
    C. those with two healthy genes
    D. A and B
    E. B and C
    F. any of the above

5. Lenny is a very active toddler who began to crawl, pull himself up to a standing position, walk, climb, and run at a very early age. Constantly chasing him and keeping him safe has made his parents very tired and stressed. As a result, they have gated off much of their home, only allowing Lenny to be in one nearly empty room (with a parent, of course) for a good part of the day. This is an example of the influence of a:
    A. child's genotype on his or her phenotype.
    B. child's environment on his or her phenotype.
    C. child's phenotype on his or her environment.
    D. parent's genotype on her child's genotype.

6. Behavior geneticists believe that _____ of human beings' behavioral traits are influenced at least to some degree by environmental factors.
   A. none
   B. a small percentage
   C. about half of
   D. all

7. An adoption twin study is conducted to examine the role of genetics and environment on musical ability. Which of the following results would lead to a conclusion that environmental factors are NOT very important in determining an individual's musical ability?
   A. Identical twins who were reared together are *more* similar in musical ability than identical twins who were reared apart.
   B. Identical twins who were reared together are *no* more similar in musical ability than identical twins who were reared apart.
   C. Fraternal twins reared apart are *more* similar in musical ability than identical twins reared apart.
   D. None of the above would lead to this conclusion.

8. Findings that genetic factors have less influence on IQ before adolescence than during adulthood are indicative of which of the following?
   A. genotype-phenotype association
   B. genotype-parental genotype association
   C. phenotype-environment association
   D. parental genotype-environment association

9. Heritability estimates tell us nothing about:
   A. relative contributions of genetic and environmental factors in the development of a trait in a particular individual.
   B. the differences between groups on a particular trait.
   C. the extent to which a trait is immutable.
   D. any of the above.

10. The degree of similarity between adoptive (genetically unrelated but reared together) siblings is attributed to their:
    A. shared genetics.
    B. nonshared genetics.
    C. shared environment.
    D. nonshared environment.

11. Which part of the neuron outputs information to other neurons?
   A. axon
   B. synapse
   C. dendrite
   D. cell body

12. Which lobe of the cerebral cortex is most important for spatial processing?
   A. temporal
   B. parietal
   C. frontal
   D. occipital

13. The two hemispheres of the brain are specialized for different modes of processing, a phenomenon referred to as:
   A. frontal lobe management.
   B. corpus callosum communication.
   C. cerebral lateralization.
   D. association area specialization.

14. Myelin serves as:
   A. insulation.
   B. connective tissue.
   C. path for communication.
   D. the cell body for some neurons.

15. The fact that babies with a "lazy eye," if it goes untreated, can become blind in the non-dominant eye demonstrates the:
   A. importance of experience in synaptic elimination and preservation.
   B. random nature of neuron creation.
   C. inability of infants and toddlers to coordinate the sensory information received from the eyes.
   D. fact that nature is more important than nurture when it comes to brain development.

16. During which of the following processes is brain damage *least* likely to lead to permanent deficiencies?
   A. neurogenesis
   B. neuron migration
   C. synaptogenesis
   D. Sustaining brain damage during any of the above are equally likely to lead to permanent deficiencies.

17. Which of the following is NOT a factor involved in nonorganic failure-to-thrive?
   A. infant's lack of interest in food
   B. mother's frustration at not being able to get her baby to eat
   C. infant's inability to stay awake to eat
   D. All of the above are factors.

18. Newborns prefer which of the following tastes?
   A. bland
   B. sweet
   C. spicy
   D. sour
   E. None of the above. Newborns have no taste preferences.

19. Which of the following pairs is likely to be most similar in weight?
   A. fraternal twins reared together
   B. fraternal twins reared apart
   C. identical twins reared apart
   D. adopted children and their adoptive parents

20. Which of the following is an *indirect* effect of malnutrition?
   A. brain damage
   B. illness
   C. minimal exploration of the environment
   D. delayed physical growth

Essay Questions

Instructions: Answer the following essay questions on a separate sheet of paper.

1. Describe the concept of an X-linked disorder. Are males and females equally susceptible to these types of disorders? Why or why not?

2. Think about a trait or characteristic you possess that you are particularly proud to possess. Using the relations that are involved in the model of hereditary and environmental influence, discuss how you may have developed this trait or characteristic. Specifically, (1) How might your parents' genotype have directly influenced your genotype? (2) How might your parents' phenotype have influenced your environment? (3) How might your phenotype have evoked your parents' behavior toward you? and (4) How did you actively select your own environment?

3. Your friend reads an article about a twin study conducted to examine the heritability of mathematical intelligence. The article reports a heritability estimate of 55%. Your friend says, "See, this is why men are better at math and science than women." Is your friend's conclusion correct? Discuss why or why not.

4. Why do you think the text book singled out the cerebral cortex as the part of the brain on which to focus? What is special about the cortex?

5. Describe how synaptogenesis and synapse elimination work together in the development of the brain.

Answer Key

Key Term Matching I

1. g	9. j	17. m	25. r	33. u	41. xx	49. ss
2. i	10. l	18. t	26. bb	34. mm	42. kk	50. oo
3. n	11. h	19. dd	27. x	35. vv	43. jj	51. nn
4. c	12. p	20. v	28. gg	36. qq	44. uu	
5. q	13. a	21. ee	29. w	37. pp	45. ww	
6. o	14. d	22. cc	30. s	38. tt	46. ll	
7. b	15. f	23. aa	31. z	39. hh	47. rr	
8. k	16. e	24. ff	32. y	40. yy	48. ii	

Key Term Matching II

1. i	6. b	11. a	16. g	21. aa	26. ee	31. z
2. l	7. k	12. h	17. q	22. x	27. gg	32. s
3. p	8. f	13. e	18. w	23. r	28. t	33. u
4. j	9. o	14. c	19. ff	24. v	29. hh	34. cc
5. m	10. d	15. n	20. bb	25. dd	30. y	

True/False Questions

1. F	6. T	11. T	16. T
2. T	7. F	12. F	17. T
3. F	8. T	13. T	18. F
4. T	9. F	14. F	19. F
5. T	10. T	15. F	20. F

Multiple-Choice Questions

1. B	6. D	11. A	16. C
2. D	7. B	12. B	17. D
3. C	8. C	13. C	18. B
4. D	9. D	14. A	19. C
5. C	10. C	15. A	20. C

CHAPTER 4
Theories of Cognitive Development

Learning Objectives

Following the completion of the study of Chapter 4, you should be able to:

1. Describe Piaget's view of children's nature.

2. Explain sources of continuity and discontinuity in Piaget's theory, applying the concepts of **assimilation**, **accommodation**, and **stages**.

3. Describe the approximate age and the new ways of knowing that characterize each of Piaget's four stages of cognitive development.

4. Describe the present assessment of Piaget's theory, incorporating both the strengths and limitations of the theory.

5. Describe the view of children's nature embodied in information-processing theories.

6. Name the basic processes that underlie information processing.

7. Summarize the contributions of strategies and content knowledge to developmental changes in memory and learning.

8. Explain the distinctions between traditional information-processing approaches and a) connectionist theories, b) dynamic-systems theories, and c) overlapping-waves theories.

9. Describe the view of children's nature conveyed in core-knowledge theories.

10. Explain the concept of domain specificity as used in core-knowledge theories.

11. Describe the view of children's nature conveyed in sociocultural theories.

12. Explain the concept of **guided participation**, incorporating the concepts of **zone of proximal development, intersubjectivity**, and **social scaffolding.**

13. Compare the four theories presented in this chapter with regard to the central development issues with which they are most concerned.

14. Apply concepts from each of the four major theoretical approaches to everyday observations and interactions with children.

You Should Know:

Piaget's Theory (*summary on pg. 143 of text*)

View of Children's Nature
- Piaget's central assumptions about children and their learning.

Central Developmental Issues
- Piaget's view on the interaction of nature and nurture and on the continuities and discontinuities in cognitive development.
- the central properties of Piaget's stage theory.
- the general manners of thinking (as well as the ages) of children in each stage.
- why children in each stage think differently.

The Sensorimotor Stage (Birth to 2 Years)
- how infants' thinking proceeds through six substages.
- how infants' intelligence is characterized within each substage, including their abilities and the limitations of their thinking within each substage.

The Preoperational Stage (Ages 2 to 7)
- how young children's thinking is characterized, including their abilities and their limitations.
- how Piaget tested young children's thinking with specifically-designed tasks, how children in this stage generally perform, and how Piaget interpreted their performance as an indication of cognitive limitations.

The Concrete Operations Stage (Ages 7 to 12)
- how older children's thinking is characterized, including their abilities and their limitations.
- how Piaget tested older children's thinking with specifically-designed tasks and how children in this stage generally perform.

The Formal Operations Stage (Ages 12 and Beyond)
- how adolescents who have reached this stage are able to think, including cognitive abilities they did not have in the concrete operations stage.
- how the behavior of individuals in this stage differs from the behavior of children in the concrete operations stage when it comes to scientific experiments.

Box 4.1 Applications: Educational Applications of Piaget's Theory
- how Piaget's theory can inform educational practices.

- how Piaget's theory has been applied to teach children about the concept of speed.

Piaget's Legacy

- the strengths of Piaget's theory and how it has influenced current thinking about cognitive development.
- the most important weaknesses of Piaget's theory and how alternative theories are attempts to overcome these weaknesses.

Information-Processing Theories (*summary on pg. 155 of text*)

Introduction

- the distinctive features of information-processing theories.
- how problem solving and memory are associated.

View of Children's Nature

- where this approach stands on the continuity-discontinuity and active-passive dimensions and why.
- how this approach envisions children's cognition and how it explains development.

Central Developmental Issues

- why memory is considered an important aspect of cognition and what the three main components of memory are, how they relate to one another, and how they develop.
- how and why basic processes, strategies, and content knowledge change with development and how they influence memory development and learning.
- what types of information children and adults tend to encode.
- how autobiographical memory develops and what explanations for infantile amnesia have been proposed.
- how the overlapping-waves approach depicts the development of problem solving and why strategic variability is beneficial.
- how planning and analogical reasoning develop and influence problem solving and why young children sometimes fail to plan.
- how the dynamic-systems perspective builds upon and differs from the traditional information-processing approach and how this perspective views the A-Not-B error.

Box 4.2 Applications: Educational Applications of Information-Processing Theories

- how information-processing theories can inform educational practices.
- how analysis of children's errors can help them learn.

Core-Knowledge Theories (*summary on pg. 160 of text*)

Introduction
- the characteristics common to core-knowledge theories.

View of Children's Nature
- the general manner of children's thinking according to this approach.
- where this approach stands on its view of children's innate abilities and how this differs from Piaget's theory and information-processing theories.
- how research supports the existence of specialized learning mechanisms.

Central Developmental Issues
- the characteristics of children's innate understandings and in which domains these understandings occur.
- the characteristics of children's informal theories and why children form these theories in the domains in which they do.
- when children first possess core theories, how research supports their existence, and how development beyond these initial theories proceeds.

Box 4.3 Applications: Educational Applications of Core-Knowledge Theories
- how core-knowledge theories can inform educational practices.
- how children's use of personification can help and hinder their understanding of biology.

Sociocultural Theories (*summary on pg. 166 of text*)

Introduction
- the focus of sociocultural theories' perspective on cognitive development.
- how sociocultural theories differ from the other theories in terms of the level of emphasis on the child as an active contributor to his or her own development.
- how children learn, as well as what factors influence learning and learning opportunities, according to this approach.

View of Children's Nature
- how Vygotsky's portrayal of children differs from that of Piaget.
- where this approach stands on the continuity-discontinuity dimension and why.
- how sociocultural theories view humans as unique among animals and as products of their culture.

Central Developmental Issues

- how cognitive change occurs, according to this approach.

- how communication plays a key role in learning and what characteristics of communication facilitate this role.

- how more competent individuals facilitate learning in less competent individuals and how this facilitation differs according to the competence of the less competent individual.

Box 4.4 Applications: Educational Applications of Sociocultural Theories

- how sociocultural theories can inform educational practices.

- what the community-of-learners program is and what benefits it has.

Key Term Matching I: Definitions

Instructions: Match each key term with its definition.

Set A

KEY TERM

1. _____ infantile amnesia
2. _____ selective attention
3. _____ guided participation
4. _____ conservation concept
5. _____ encoding
6. _____ overlapping-waves theory
7. _____ organization
8. _____ deferred imitation
9. _____ preoperational stage
10. _____ intersubjectivity
11. _____ zone of proximal development

12. _____ autobiographical memory
13. _____ rehearsal
14. _____ adaptation
15. _____ concrete operational stage
16. _____ memory
17. _____ formal operational stage
18. _____ sensorimotor stage
19. _____ dynamic-systems theories
20. _____ core-knowledge theories
21. _____ symbolic representation
22. _____ task analysis

DEFINITION

a. the replication of another person's behavior a considerable amount of time after it has been observed

b. the process of representing in memory information that is considered important

c. Piaget's stage in which intelligence is developed and expressed through sensory and motor abilities

d. an information-processing approach that emphasizes how variable children's thinking is

e. Piaget's stage in which intelligence becomes logical, but not abstract

f. a process by which more knowledgeable individuals organize situations to enable less knowledgeable individuals to learn

g. the tendency to react to the demands of the environment in ways that meet one's goals

h. the use of one object to signify another

i. the range of performance between what children can do unsupported and what they can do when they have the best possible support

j. the identification of goals, relevant information in the environment, and potential processing strategies

k. the tendency to integrate particular observations into coherent knowledge

l. the process of repeating information again and again in order to assist oneself in remembering it

m. the process of intentionally focusing on the information that is most relevant to the current goal while ignoring other information

n. the failure to remember very early experiences

o. knowledge of the events of one's life

p. an information-processing approach that emphasizes how various aspects of the individual function as a unified whole to produce behavior

q. Piaget's stage in which intelligence begins to develop through language and symbolic thought

r. approaches to cognitive development that focus on the sophistication of children's thinking in areas that have had evolutionary importance

s. Piaget's stage in which intelligence enables individuals to think abstractly and hypothetically

t. the mutual understanding that individuals share during communication

u. the knowledge that changes in the appearance of objects do not alter their fundamental properties

v. the retention of information over time

Set B

KEY TERM

23. _____ working memory		33. _____ object permanence	
24. _____ centration		34. _____ A-Not-B error	
25. _____ joint attention		35. _____ domain specific	
26. _____ accommodation		36. _____ long-term memory	
27. _____ equilibration		37. _____ assimilation	
28. _____ sociocultural theories		38. _____ social referencing	
29. _____ basic processes		39. _____ utilization deficiency	
30. _____ cultural tools		40. _____ egocentrism	
31. _____ social scaffolding		41. _____ sensory memory	
32. _____ problem solving		42. _____ personification	

DEFINITION

w.   the tendency to focus solely on a single feature of an object or event

x.   sights, sounds, and other sensations that are just entering the cognitive system and are held briefly in raw form

y.   the process by which assimilation and accommodation are balanced to create a stable understanding

z.   a process by which more competent people provide a temporary framework that supports children's thinking at a more advanced level than they could manage on their own

aa.   the tendency to reach for objects where they have been found previously, rather than where they were most recently hidden

bb.   the products of human ingenuity that enhance thinking

cc.   the process by which individuals interpret incoming information into a form they can understand

dd.   predicting the qualities of other animals from knowledge about humans

ee.   the simplest and most frequently used mental activities

ff.   the phenomenon that early uses of memory strategies are not as successful as later uses gg.   where information from sensory memory and long-term memory come together to be actively processed

hh.   the process by which individuals adapt their current understandings in response to new information

ii.   information retained on an enduring basis

jj.   limited to a particular topic

kk.   the process of using a strategy to overcome an obstacle and thus achieve a goal

ll.   approaches to cognitive development that emphasize the interpersonal context in which development occurs

mm.   the tendency to perceive the world solely from one's own view

nn.   a process in which individuals intentionally focus on the same external stimulus during communication

oo.   the tendency to look to others for guidance about how to respond to unfamiliar or threatening events

pp.   the knowledge that objects continue to exist even when they are out of view

Key Term Matching II: Applications, Examples, and More

Instructions: Match each key term with an application or example of the term.

Set A

KEY TERM

1. _____ conservation concept	11. _____ deferred imitation
2. _____ rehearsal	12. _____ dynamic-systems theories
3. _____ sensorimotor stage	13. _____ infantile amnesia
4. _____ memory	14. _____ core-knowledge theories
5. _____ selective attention	15. _____ encoding
6. _____ guided participation	16. _____ intersubjectivity
7. _____ concrete operational stage	17. _____ symbolic representation
8. _____ formal operational stage	18. _____ overlapping-waves theories
9. _____ zone of proximal development	19. _____ autobiographical memory
10. _____ preoperational stage	20. _____ task analysis

APPLICATION OR EXAMPLE

a.   social scaffolding allows children to perform at the high end of this

b.   individuals in this stage of Piaget's theory have object permanence, but do not have a conservation concept

c.   research indicating that children simultaneously possess multiple arithmetic strategies, some more mature than others, lends support for this information-processing approach

d.   individuals in this stage of Piaget's theory can think deeply about concepts such as freedom and morality

e.   a father who shows his son how to turn all of the puzzle pieces in the correct direction and suggests that his son put together the outside pieces first is engaging in this

f.   information-processing theorists attempt to understand and predict individuals' behavior with this

g.   this limits very young children's use of autobiographical memory in recognizing events that should be familiar

h.   a child who picks up a block, holds it to his ear, and says, "Hello?" is demonstrating his capacity for this

i.   this occurs automatically for some information, such as data on the relative frequency of events, but children fail to do this for other important information

j.   this helps children separate fact from fiction, as in the example of children being asked outlandish questions about common events

k.   an individual who says a phone number repeatedly between the time she looks it up in the phone book and the time she dials the number is engaging in this

l.   a child who intentionally focuses solely on the spelling of words on her spelling list while ignoring the definitions of the words is engaging in this memory strategy

m.   problem solving and this work together to help children attain their goals

n.   operating under this approach, researchers have demonstrated how the A-Not-B error is not simply an indication of incomplete conceptual understanding, but is associated with motor activities and attention as well

o.   individuals in this stage of Piaget's theory would be unlikely to give their daddy a pacifier if he gets hurt, but would still be unable to perform systematic scientific experiments

p.   theorists who support this approach believe that individuals are born with specialized learning abilities in domains such as identifying human faces and language learning

q.   a child who observes her father turn on the oven and then tries to turn the knob herself the following day is engaging in this

r.   this is unlikely without joint attention

s.   for much of the time individuals spend in this stage of Piaget's theory, they have no understanding that objects continue to exist when out of their view

t.   a child who watches a line of closely-spaced pennies as they are spread out and believes that there are more pennies after they are spread out does NOT possess knowledge of this

Set B

KEY TERM

21. _____ object permanence
22. _____ cultural tools
23. _____ working memory
24. _____ sociocultural theories
25. _____ problem solving
26. _____ long-term memory
27. _____ A-Not-B error
28. _____ joint attention
29. _____ egocentrism
30. _____ social scaffolding

31. _____ assimilation
32. _____ domain specific
33. _____ basic processes
34. _____ accommodation
35. _____ utilization deficiency
36. _____ social referencing
37. _____ centration
38. _____ personification
39. _____ sensory memory

APPLICATION OR EXAMPLE

u. even infants have these mental abilities, but children are able to execute these more efficiently with age

v. an infant who realizes that a beach ball cannot be grabbed in the same way as her favorite rattle and thus grabs the ball with two hands has engaged in this process

w. this is also referred to as short-term memory

x. a child who searches for a ball that rolled behind a door, even though it has previously been found several times under the table, is NOT having this problem

y. core-knowledge theorists believe that learning mechanisms have this characteristic

z. examples of these are the symbol systems, artifacts, skills, and values that are part of the broad contexts in which interactions take place

aa. key to information-processing theories is the assumption that children are actively engaged in this when they are trying to achieve goals

bb. an infant who tries to grab a beach ball in the same way she has previously grabbed her favorite rattle has engaged in this process

cc. children whose early attempts to use rehearsal are unsuccessful are meeting this problem

dd. this concept requires the ability to mentally represent objects ee.   information is held here for a fraction of a second

ff.   an example of this is a child's knowledge about animals

gg.   Piaget used the three-mountains task to demonstrate this

hh.   by its very nature, this teaching behavior becomes less extensive as children learn to complete a particular task on their own

ii.   theorists who support this approach place less emphasis than do other theorists on the active role children play in their own development and a greater emphasis on the role of others

jj.   individuals must progress past this tendency in order to succeed at a conservation task

kk.   a mother who points to an airplane and says, "Look at the airplane," to her baby is counting on this in order for the baby to learn

ll.   a way in which children actively seek out the reactions of their social partners when faced with unfamiliar events

mm.   a child who believes that squirrels have tables and chairs at which to eat their acorns is demonstrating this practice

True/False Questions

Instructions: Indicate whether each item is true or false.

_____ 1. In Piaget's preoperational stage, children first acquire the ability to learn through the process of equilibration.

_____ 2. According to Piaget, infants' ability to find a hidden object even when its location has been changed develops at a younger age than the ability to imitate another person's behavior well after it has occurred.

_____ 3. According to Piagetian theory, most five-year-olds can solve conservation-of-number problems and conservation-of-solid-quantity problems, but are unable to solve conservation-of-liquid-quantity problems.

_____ 4. The pendulum problem described in the text is typically used with preschool-age children.

_____ 5. A criticism of Piaget's theory is that too much emphasis is placed on the influence of the social world on the development of children's thinking.

_____ 6. Working memory can typically hold information for 1/3 of a second, and then retention falls sharply.

_____ 7. People encode all of the information that they see and hear.

_____ 8. Biological maturation, along with experience, appears to contribute to the development of processing speed.

_____ 9. The strategy of repeating information over and over again in order to remember it is referred to as autobiographical memory.

_____ 10. Eight-year-olds are only slightly better than four-year-olds at using the strategy of selective attention.

_____ 11. Children who have knowledge about a particular subject can often remember new information about that subject better than can adults who have less prior knowledge.

_____ 12. Infantile amnesia generally involves memories for all events occurring prior to the age of three years and most events occurring prior to the age of five years.

_____ 13. The overlapping-waves approach views children's strategic variability as a source of delayed learning.

_____ 14. As children develop, their use of analogical reasoning requires fewer superficial similarities between the problems, and it is less likely to be impeded by superficial dissimilarities between the problems.

_____ 15. Core-knowledge theories propose that children are born with detailed understandings of several important domains.

_____   16.   The core-knowledge approach often conflicts with Piagetian theory in that Piaget overestimated young children's innate knowledge.

_____   17.   Core-knowledge theorists view children as passive learners.

_____   18.   Young children commonly use social referencing in familiar situations.

_____   19.   Joint attention facilitates language acquisition.

_____   20.   Parents tend to contribute to children's problem solving in ways that suggest that they intuitively understand the concept of the zone of proximal development.

Multiple-Choice Questions

1. Which of the following is a true statement about Piaget's beliefs about learning?
   A. Children are intrinsically motivated to learn.
   B. Children need rewards and punishments from adults to learn.
   C. Children depend on instruction from adults to learn.
   D. Children's learning occurs purely as a function of biological maturation.

2. Six-month-old Hayden has been exclusively breast-fed since birth, and thus he never has drunk milk from a bottle. The first time Hayden is offered the bottle, he tries to suck on it the same way he is used to sucking. Hayden's sucking behavior is an indication that he has engaged in which of the following processes?
   A. equilibration
   B. calibration
   C. accommodation
   D. assimilation

3. Five-year-old children are generally considered to be in which of Piaget's stages?
   A. formal operations
   B. sensorimotor
   C. postoperational
   D. preoperational
   E. concrete operations

4. Mark and his mother are playing with an interesting rattle. Mark's mother is shaking the rattle in front of him and then hiding it under a large bowl. Mark is having fun finding the rattle under the bowl and then giving it back to his mother. After several rounds of this game, Mark's mother hides the rattle in a cabinet instead of under the bowl. Rather than looking in the cabinet, however, Mark lifts the bowl to look for the rattle. Mark is probably approximately what age?
   A. 1 month old
   B. 6 months old
   C. 12 months old
   D. 18 months old

5. Repetition of other people's behavior some time after it has been observed is referred to as:
   A. formal operations.
   B. post-observation modeling.
   C. symbolic representations.
   D. deferred imitation.

6. Which of the following is an example of egocentrism?
   A. Megan picks up a block and pretends to talk into it like a phone.
   B. Jane gives her father a doll for his birthday.
   C. Matthew thinks 10 pennies are worth more than one quarter.
   D. Jing opens the cabinet to get a cup after seeing his father get a cup the previous day.

7. Raymond's mother pours a cup of milk for him and then realizes that the cup has a small crack in it. Not wanting her son to cut his lip, she pours the milk into another cup. The second cup happens to be shorter and wider than the first cup. Raymond starts crying because he thinks the second cup holds less milk than the first cup. Raymond is in which of Piaget's stages?
   A. formal operations
   B. sensorimotor
   C. postoperational
   D. preoperational
   E. concrete operations

8. Task analysis is part of which of the following theories?
   A. Core-knowledge
   B. Information-processing
   C. Piagetian
   D. Sociocultural

9. Which of the following is a true statement about sensory memory?
   A. It can retain information for an unlimited amount of time.
   B. Its capacity increases markedly through adulthood.
   C. Adults can hold between 7 and 10 pieces of information in it.
   D. None of the above is a true statement.

10. Which of the following is NOT considered a basic process by information-processing theorists?
   A. encoding specific features of objects
   B. infantile amnesia
   C. recognizing objects as familiar
   D. associating events with each other

11. Eight-year-old Jessica has a spelling test the next day. She has a spelling list, and her teacher has told her that the test will only involve the items in the first half of the list. When trying to learn the spellings of the words that will be tested, she intentionally focuses solely on the spellings of the words in the first half of the list and ignores the spellings of the words in the second half of the list, even though she knows she will be tested on those words next time. Jessica is using which of the following strategies?
    A. working memory
    B. selective attention
    C. rehearsal
    D. utilization deficiency

12. Which of the following explanations is LEAST likely to be involved in causing the end of infantile amnesia?
    A. Autobiographical memory develops through parents discussing past events with children.
    B. The frontal lobe of the brain develops considerably during this period.
    C. Pre-verbal children encode experiences in a way that cannot be translated into verbal terms.
    D. During this period, children develop a sense of self.

13. Analogical reasoning involves which of the following?
    A. understanding new problems in terms of familiar ones
    B. planning a strategy to solve a problem
    C. testing several strategies to determine which will work
    D. completing a task analysis
    E. all of the above

14. Which of the following is a key difference between Piaget's theory and core-knowledge theories?
    A. depiction of children as active versus passive learners
    B. view of the types of learning abilities that are innate
    C. focus on the importance of nature versus nurture
    D. expectation of the motivation involved in cognitive development

15. According to core-knowledge theories, informal theories of which of the following domains develop earliest?
    A. psychology
    B. biology
    C. physics
    D. Informal theories of all of the above domains are fully developed at birth.

16. Randy tells his mother that their cow is happy that they are drinking her milk. This is an example of:
   A. animification.
   B. objectification.
   C. emotionification.
   D. personification.

17. Which of the following is an example of guided participation?
   A. Jacob's father separates all of the large Lego pieces so Jacob will know he should start building the bridge with the large pieces.
   B. Emma's grandmother shows her how to bake cookies.
   C. Jose's teacher pairs Jose with another child who generally does not let him play in the group.
   D. Rhonda's uncle gives her explicit instructions on how to draw a house.

18. According to sociocultural theories, the processes that produce development _____ across cultures, and/but the content of what children learn _____ across cultures.
   A. are the same; is the same
   B. are the same; differs
   C. differ; is the same
   D. differ; differs

19. Joint attention is an example of:
   A. social scaffolding.
   B. guided participation.
   C. social referencing.
   D. intersubjectivity.

20. Which of the following constructs is NOT a part of sociocultural theories?
   A. intersubjectivity
   B. social scaffolding
   C. informal theories
   D. zone of proximal development

Essay Questions

Instructions: Answer the following essay questions on a separate sheet of paper.

1. Give an example of a conservation problem and describe how children in Piaget's preoperational stage, concrete operations stage, and formal operations stage would deal with the problem. What are the features of thinking in each stage that explain children's typical responses?

2. Describe three strengths and three weaknesses of Piaget's theory. For each strength and weakness, provide a specific example. In addition, for each weakness, state which alternative theory or theories (if any) discussed in the chapter addresses the weakness.

3. Consider how basic processes, strategies, and content knowledge work together to produce learning and improvements in memory with age. Describe several differences between what a young child and an older child would tend to remember after visiting a museum, and describe how differences in basic processes, strategies, and content knowledge contribute to these differences in memory and learning.

4. Imagine you are a volunteer in the "Big Brother/Big Sister" Program, and you are helping your little "sibling" with his or her math homework. Describe the cultural tools involved in this interaction and how they influence the learning situation.

5. Describe the "jigsaw approach." What are the benefits of this approach, and why is it supported by sociocultural theories? Imagine you are an elementary school teacher, and you would like to use the jigsaw approach for the topic of weather. Provide a brief description of how you would use the approach.

Answer Key

Key Term Matching I

1. n	7. k	13. l	19. p	25. nn	31. z	37. cc
2. m	8. a	14. g	20. r	26. hh	32. kk	38. oo
3. f	9. q	15. e	21. h	27. y	33. pp	39. ff
4. u	10. t	16. v	22. j	28. ll	34. aa	40. mm
5. b	11. i	17. s	23. gg	29. ee	35. jj	41. x
6. d	12. o	18. c	24. w	30. bb	36. ii	42. dd

Key Term Matching II

1. t	7. o	13. g	19. j	25. aa	31. bb	37. jj
2. k	8. d	14. p	20. f	26. ff	32. y	38. mm
3. s	9. a	15. i	21. dd	27. x	33. u	39. ee
4. m	10. b	16. r	22. z	28. kk	34. v	
5. l	11. q	17. h	23. w	29. gg	35. cc	
6. e	12. n	18. c	24. ii	30. hh	36. ll	

True/False Questions

1. F	6. T	11. T	16. F
2. T	7. F	12. T	17. F
3. F	8. T	13. F	18. F
4. F	9. F	14. T	19. T
5. F	10. F	15. F	20. T

Multiple-Choice Questions

1. A	6. B	11. B	16. D
2. D	7. D	12. D	17. A
3. D	8. B	13. A	18. B
4. C	9. D	14. B	19. D
5. D	10. B	15. C	20. C

CHAPTER 5

Infancy

Learning Objectives

Following the completion of the study of Chapter 5, you should be able to:

1. Apply theories presented previously in the course, especially Piaget's theory and core-knowledge approaches, to the understanding of perception and cognition in infancy.

2. Explain the **preferential-looking technique** for the study of infant perception.

3. Describe the rapid development of visual acuity, scanning patterns, and pattern perception that occurs during infancy.

4. Name the sources of information infants use to perceive depth and objects.

5. Provide evidence for **intermodal** perception in early infancy.

6. Demonstrate several reflexes that are present at birth.

7. Explain the role of culture and experience in the achievement of motor milestones.

8. Describe the developmental progression of reaching and self-locomotion.

9. Explain and apply to examples the following forms of infant learning: habituation/dishabituation, perceptual learning, instrumental conditioning, classical conditioning, and observational learning.

10. Explain the use of the violation-of-expectancy procedure in the study of infant cognition.

11. Compare the results of recent research on infants' object concept using the violation-of-expectancy procedure with expectations based on Piaget's theory.

12. Explain alternative theories for the A-Not-B error.
    Describe the development of means–end problem solving in infancy.

You Should Know:

Perception (*summary on pg. 184 of text*)

Introduction
- the difference between sensation and perception.

Vision
- the methodologies used to examine infants' visual abilities and what they have demonstrated about infants' preferences and visual acuity.
- the general limitations of infant vision compared to the vision of adults.
- how infants' perception of patterns and objects develops, including how the cues used to perceive objects changes with development.
- how the cues used to perceive depth change with development and the methods used to study infants' use of these cues.

Box 5.1: Beauty and the Baby
- what factors are involved in newborns' attraction to faces, and how infants' perception of the human face develops.
- what types of faces infants prefer and how these preferences have been studied.

Box 5.2: Picture Perception
- how infants perceive and understand pictures.

Auditory Perception
- how well infants' auditory system is developed at birth.
- how infants perceive aspects of music, what their preferences are and the extent to which their musical perception is similar to that of adults.

Taste and Smell
- some of the tastes and smells preferred by infants and how these preferences are formed.

Touch
- how touch helps younger and older infants understand the world.

Intermodal Perception
- how intermodal perception has been examined in infants and what it has indicated about the developmental path of these abilities.

Motor Development *(summary on pg. 194 of text)*

Reflexes

- what reflexes are, with examples of those that have adaptive significance and those that do not appear to have any adaptive significance.

Motor Milestones

- the general age range for the major motor milestones.
- how sociocultural factors can influence the timing of major motor milestones.

Current Views of Motor Development

- how current views of motor development differ from early views, and how the dynamic-systems perspective has broadened the view of what influences motor development.

Box 5.3: "The Case of the Disappearing Reflex"

- how systematic research conducted within a dynamic-systems approach has demonstrated that multiple factors are influencing the disappearance of the stepping reflex.

The Expanding World of the Infant

- how reaching and self-produced locomotion change infants' experience of the world.
- how infants' awareness of their bodies and motor abilities, as well as their perception of the environment, influence their reaching and locomotor behaviors.
- the types of misjudgments that young children make and how this informs our understanding of their development.

Box 5.4: A Recent Secular Change in Motor Development

- how a secular change in motor development was apparently caused by a societal change.

Box 5.5: "Travel Broadens the Mind"

- how a long series of research studies has examined and demonstrated the interdependence of depth perception, fear responses, self-produced locomotion, and the social context of development.

Learning *(summary on pg. 200 of text)*

Habituation

- what the process of habituation is and why it is adaptive.
- how the speed of habituation is associated with later cognitive ability.

Perceptual Learning
- what perceptual learning is, and the key processes involved in it.
- what infants learn from paying attention to the objects and events they perceive.

Statistical Learning
- how infants learn expectancies for future events and how this has been examined.

Classical Conditioning
- what classical conditioning is and what its component stimuli and responses are.
- how classical conditioning plays a role in everyday learning and emotional responses.

Instrumental Conditioning
- what instrumental conditioning is and what the limitations on learning in this fashion are.
- how learning through instrumental conditioning also teaches infants about their impact on their environment.

Observational Learning
- what observational learning is and how it develops with age.
- how children's understanding of intention plays a role in their observational learning.

Cognition (*summary on pg. 207 of text*)

Introduction
- how different theoretical perspectives point to different sources of infants' cognitive abilities.

Object Knowledge
- Piaget's perspective on infants' knowledge of objects and conceptions of object permanence.
- how more recent research using two different methodologies has demonstrated more advanced knowledge of object permanence than the research concluded by Piaget.
- how the violation-of-expectancy paradigm has been used to examine a variety of expectations about objects by infants.
- how research has led to a number of explanations for infants' A-Not-B error.

Physical Knowledge
- how infants' physical knowledge, including an understanding of gravity, develops.

- how a series of studies using the violation-of-expectancy procedure has demonstrated infants' developing understanding of object-support relations.

Social Knowledge

- what infants appear to know about people and their behavior and how research has demonstrated this knowledge.

- how infants appear able to use their social knowledge in their interactions with other people.

Key Term Matching I: Definitions

Instructions: Match each key term with its definition.

Set A

KEY TERM

1. _____ unconditioned stimulus
2. _____ stepping reflex
3. _____ fovea
4. _____ conditioned response
5. _____ intermodal perception
6. _____ scale errors
7. _____ prereaching movements
8. _____ preferential-looking technique

9. _____ violation-of-expectancy
10. _____ self-locomotion
11. _____ unconditioned response
12. _____ conditioned stimulus
13. _____ auditory localization
14. _____ instrumental conditioning
15. _____ positive reinforcement
16. _____ classical conditioning

DEFINITION

a. a method for studying whether infants have a liking for one object or pattern over another that involves showing infants two patterns or two objects simultaneously

b. an attempt by a young child to perform an action on a miniature object that is impossible due to the large discrepancy in size between the child and the object

c. in classical conditioning, a neutral stimulus that comes to evoke the response by being repeatedly paired with the original stimulus

d. in classical conditioning, the response that was initially reflexive but comes to be elicited by the conditioned stimulus

e. a form of learning that involves associating one's own behavior with its consequences

f. a neonatal reflex in which infants move their legs in a coordinated pattern like walking

g. in classical conditioning, a reflexive response that is evoked by the unconditioned stimulus

h. in classical conditioning, a stimulus that evokes a reflexive response

i.   a procedure used to study infant cognition that involves showing infants an event designed to evoke surprise or interest if it goes against something the infant knows or assumes to be true

j.   a reward that consistently follows a particular behavior and increases the likelihood of the behavior being repeated

k.   infants' clumsy swiping movements in the general vicinity of objects

l.   the central region of the retina

m.   the perception of the location of a sound source

n.   the combining of information from two or more sensory systems

o.   the ability to move oneself around in the environment

p.   a form of learning that involves associating an initially neutral stimulus with a stimulus that always evokes a particular reflexive response

Set B

KEY TERM

17. _____ sensation

18. _____ optical expansion

19. _____ binocular disparity

20. _____ reflexes

21. _____ social referencing

22. _____ object segregation

23. _____ perception

24. _____ visual acuity

25. _____ stereopsis

26. _____ pictorial cues

27. _____ contrast sensitivity

28. _____ perceptual constancy

29. _____ differentiation

30. _____ affordances

DEFINITION

q. the possibilities for action offered by objects and situations

r. the depth cues that can be perceived by one eye alone

s. the sharpness of visual discrimination

t. the ability to detect differences in light and dark areas of a visual pattern

u. innate, fixed patterns of action that occur in response to particular stimulation

v. the difference in the retinal image of an object in each eye that results in slightly different signals being sent to the brain

w. a depth cue in which an approaching object obscures more and more of the background

x. the perception of the boundaries between objects in a visual display

y. the pulling out of those elements that are stable from the constantly changing environment

z. the processing of basic information from the external world by the eyes, ears, skin, tongue, etc., and the brain

aa. the perception of objects as being stable in size, shape, etc., in spite of physical differences in the retinal size of the object

bb. the use of another person's emotional reaction to interpret an ambiguous situation

cc. the process by which the visual cortex computes the degree of discrepancy between the two images caused by binocular disparity

dd. the process of organizing and interpreting sensory information

Key Term Matching II: Applications, Examples, and More

Instructions: Match each key term with an application or example of the term.

Set A

KEY TERM

1. _____ stepping reflex

2. _____ auditory localization

3. _____ conditioned stimulus

4. _____ violation-of-expectancy

5. _____ self-locomotion

6. _____ instrumental conditioning

7. _____ preferential-looking technique

8. _____ unconditioned response

9. _____ intermodal perception

10. _____ conditioned response

11. _____ classical conditioning

12. _____ positive reinforcement

13. _____ unconditioned stimulus

APPLICATION OR EXAMPLE

a. with this method, if infants look at one pattern for a longer duration than they look at another pattern, researchers conclude that infants can distinguish between the two patterns

b. if her parents' clapping after she dances increases the likelihood that a toddler will dance in the future, the clapping is considered this

c. in the example of the infant who has learned to cry at the mere sight of a doctor because of repeated pairings of the doctor and the pain of vaccinations, the crying as a result of seeing the doctor is termed this

d. cortical maturation was ruled out as the cause of the disappearance of this by the examination of multiple factors such as leg weight and strength

e. in the example of the infant who has learned to cry at the mere sight of a doctor because of repeated pairings of the doctor and the pain of vaccinations, the crying as a result of the injection is termed this

f. with this procedure, infants are expected to look longer at an "impossible" event (such as, a screen appearing to rotate through a solid object) than at a "possible" event (such as, a screen that stops rotating at the location in which it would hit the solid object)

g. in the example of the infant who has learned to cry at the mere sight of a doctor because of repeated pairings of the doctor and the pain of vaccinations, the injection is termed this

h.   Campos and his colleagues demonstrated that this plays a vital role in the development of fear of heights

i.   in the example of the infant who has learned to cry at the mere sight of a doctor because of repeated pairings of the doctor and the pain of vaccinations, the sight of the doctor is termed this

j.   infants' ability to pick out the video that is synchronized with the audio they are hearing is evidence of auditory-visual _____

k.   a toddler who now understands that others will clap when she dances has learned this through this type of learning

l.   newborns' ability to do this is demonstrated by their turning toward a sound

m.   an infant who begins to cry at the mere sight of a doctor has learned to associate the doctor with the pain of vaccinations as a result of this type of learning

Set B

KEY TERM

14. _____ binocular disparity   20. _____ sensation

15. _____ differentiation   21. _____ stereopsis

16. _____ visual acuity   22. _____ object segregation

17. _____ contrast sensitivity   23. _____ reflexes

18. _____ perceptual constancy   24. _____ perception

19. _____ pictorial cues   25. _____ scale errors

APPLICATION OR EXAMPLE

n.   this is poor in infants, and thus only very different shades can be differentiated

o.   an example of this process is the experience of the taste and smell of peas evoked by the individual eating them

p.   some of these, such as rooting, have clear adaptive value, whereas others, like the tonic neck, have no known adaptive significance

q.   an example of this process is the activation of taste receptors on the tongue and receptors in the nose by the molecules in peas

r.   this process is infants' way of searching for order and regularity in the environment

s.   independent movement of objects is an important facet to infants' perception of this

t.   our brains use the degree of this as a depth cue – the greater it is, the closer the object must be, and vice versa

u.   the maturation of the visual cortex is required for this; thus, binocular disparity cannot be used as a depth cue until infants are about four months of age

v.   a child who tries to sit in his matchbox car is demonstrating this

w.   this can be assessed in infants by determining the smallest black and white stripes that they are able to distinguish from a gray square

x.   as a result of this phenomenon, infants perceive their mother as remaining stable in size despite the fact that their retinal image of her becomes larger as she walks toward them

y.   these include relative size and interposition

True/False Questions

Instructions: Indicate whether each item is true or false.

_____ 1. The preferential-looking technique can be used to examine infants' visual acuity.

_____ 2. Newborns' color vision is very poor in comparison to that of adults.

_____ 3. Three-month-old infants tend to focus their visual attention on the outer edges of objects.

_____ 4. The process of stereopsis enables individuals to use optical expansion as a cue to depth.

_____ 5. Infants can differentiate between a consonant version and a dissonant version of a piece of music, and they prefer the consonant version.

_____ 6. Sensitivity to taste and smell develops before birth.

_____ 7. Infants integrate their visual and tactile experience at a later age than they integrate their visual and oral experience.

_____ 8. The presence of reflexes at the developmentally appropriate ages is indicative of a healthy central nervous system, whereas the presence of the same reflexes at the inappropriate ages can indicate a neurological problem.

_____ 9. Infants in urban China, who are typically placed on beds surrounded by pillows to keep them off the dirty floor, are still able to crawl at the same average age as infants who are given more opportunities to crawl.

_____ 10. Until the age of eight months, infants rely on vision for accurate reaching.

_____ 11. Infants need to integrate perceptual information with each new motor behavior they develop, and thus appear unable to transfer what they had learned from their experience crawling down slopes to walking down them.

_____ 12. Scale errors are an example of failure in the integration of perception and action.

_____ 13. Habituation requires the ability to form memories.

_____ 14. Detecting predictable patterns of events is key to statistical learning.

_____ 15. Classical conditioning involves learning about the consequences of one's own behavior.

_____ 16. Infants pay attention to the intention of their models when imitating them.

_____ 17. Core-knowledge theorists believe that infants are born with detailed knowledge about the physical world.

_____ 18. Research examining infants' ability to reason about objects in the dark has supported Piaget's view of infants' object knowledge.

_____   19.   At three months of age, infants are surprised if an object released in midair remains suspended in midair.

_____   20.   Infants as young as five months old apparently interpret adults' reaching behavior as goal-directed.

Multiple-Choice Questions

1. The habituation technique is based on the expectation that infants:
   A. look longer at objects they like or find interesting.
   B. look away from complicated or frightening objects.
   C. recognize patterns they have seen on previous occasions.
   D. lose interest in objects that are familiar.

2. A seven-month-old who is perceiving a subjective contour in a visual stimulus is:
   A. detecting a shape or object that can be seen by integrating only the overall pattern.
   B. perceiving differences in the sizes of circular objects.
   C. isolating the separate elements of a display.
   D. distinguishing between two-dimensional and three-dimensional objects.

3. Perceptual constancy enables individuals to do which of the following?
   A. recognize moving point-light displays as a person walking
   B. detect an illusory square from only four cut-out corners
   C. realize that the coffee cup in our current view is the same as the one we viewed prior to blinking
   D. perceive that the building across the street is very large although the image on our retina is small

4. For which of the following depth perception cues are both eyes necessary?
   A. pictorial cues
   B. binocular disparity
   C. relative size
   D. optical expansion

5. At what age are children able to localize sounds?
   A. at birth
   B. 6 months
   C. 12 months
   D. 18 months

6. An infant is placed in a crib that vibrates to a particular rhythm. At the same time, she views two television monitors on which a bunny jumps in two different rhythms, one that matches the vibration she is experiencing and one that does not match it. If she prefers to look at the monitor showing the bunny jumping to the matching rhythm, she has detected the similarity through which of the following?
   A. visual interaction
   B. proprioceptive perception
   C. intermodal perception
   D. inter-visual recognition

7. Newborn Seth feels something touch his left cheek, and he turns his head toward that side in response. Seth has just demonstrated which reflex?
   A. rooting
   B. tonic neck
   C. sucking
   D. grasping

8. The research by Thelen in which infants were immersed waist-deep in a tank of water was designed to examine which of the following?
   A. effect of weightlessness on reaching
   B. effect of weightlessness on posture control
   C. emergence of the swimming reflex
   D. disappearance of the stepping reflex

9. Campos and his colleagues demonstrated which of the following about non-crawlers' and experienced crawlers' heart rates when they were lowered over the deep side of the visual cliff?
   A. Non-crawlers show heart-rate acceleration.
   B. Non-crawlers show no change in heart rate.
   C. Experienced crawlers show heart-rate acceleration.
   D. Experienced crawlers show no change in heart rate.

10. An infant's sibling always jumps off his bed with a loud bang when he wakes up from his nap. He then comes downstairs and greets the infant with a tickle, making the infant laugh and cough reflexively. Eventually, the infant begins to laugh and cough reflexively when he hears the bang, even before he sees his brother. The infant has learned to expect his brother's arrival through which type of learning?
    A. perceptual learning
    B. classical conditioning
    C. observational learning
    D. instrumental conditioning

11. An infant is given a pacifier that causes music to be played from a nearby speaker whenever it is sucked in a particular pattern. At first, the infant's sucking pattern is random, but she eventually learns to suck with only that pattern in order to keep the music playing. The infant has learned this through which type of learning?
    A. classical conditioning
    B. perceptual learning
    C. observational learning
    D. instrumental conditioning

12. Parents who are concerned about their children learning to behave violently by watching violent acts on television are probably most concerned about which of the following?
    A. observational learning
    B. habituation
    C. instrumental conditioning
    D. intermodal perception

13. Object permanence refers to the conception that:
    A. objects do not exist when one cannot act on them.
    B. one is unable to act on many objects because of their size or weight.
    C. objects exist independently of one's ability to perceive or act on them.
    D. large objects, such as buildings and mountains, cannot disappear.

14. A six-month-old infant is struggling to reach a colorful rattle that is on the floor in front of her. The infant's mother mistakenly drops a blanket over the rattle, concealing it from the infant. Which of the following is the infant's *most* likely response?
    A. crying at her inability to reach the rattle
    B. laughing at the fact that she can no longer see the object
    C. reaching to uncover the rattle
    D. looking away from the covered rattle and instead picking up another nearby toy

15. Research examining infants' behavior when the room becomes dark after they are shown an attractive object demonstrated which of the following?
    A. Young infants are fearful of the dark.
    B. Young infants do not expect the object to still be there when the light is turned back on again.
    C. Young infants reach for the object even when they cannot see it.
    D. Young infants respond differently to possible and impossible events.

16. Which of the following techniques is based on the expectation that infants are surprised at events that are inconsistent with their knowledge?
  A. visual preference
  B. violation-of-expectancy
  C. habituation
  D. A-Not-B error

17. Baillargeon's research in which a screen rotated 180 degrees was founded on the expectation that infants:
  A. need visual cues to determine the presence or absence of objects.
  B. will look longer at an event if they believe it to be impossible.
  C. have an innate understanding of gravity.
  D. understand the people behave in ways consistent with their goals.

18. Which of the following makes it *more* likely that infants will make the A-Not-B error?
  A. keeping the appearance of the locations distinct
  B. shortening the delay between A and B trials
  C. hiding the toy in location A on multiple trials
  D. allowing the infant to search immediately after the toy is hidden at B

19. Which of the following is the most advanced concept infants develop as they learn about support events?
  A. type of contact
  B. whether or not there is contact
  C. shape of supported object
  D. amount of contact

20. Research in which two year olds watched a desirable toy being placed on a high shelf while their parent was either in the room watching or was out of the room suggested which of the following?
  A. Children can understand their own goals, but have difficulty interpreting others' goals.
  B. Children tend to attribute goals and intentions to inanimate objects.
  C. Children can make inferences about what a person will do based on their knowledge of what the person knows.
  D. Children are able to use their understanding about what other people know.

Essay Questions

Instructions: Answer the following essay questions on a separate sheet of paper.

1. How do babies' object segregation abilities help them learn? Give examples to support your point.

2. Design a study to examine whether six-month-old infants favor happy faces to sad faces. Discuss the methodology you would use and what data you would need to conclude that they preferred happy faces.

3. Describe the role of visual perception in the development of reaching and self-locomotion.

4. Describe the following types of learning: classical conditioning, instrumental conditioning, and observational learning. Give an example of something a six-month-old infant might learn through each type.

5. The series of studies conducted by Baillargeon and her colleagues using the rotating screen has provided useful information about infants' ability to mentally represent objects. Describe these studies, including the methodology and the conclusions.

Answer Key

Key Term Matching I

1. h	6. b	11. g	16. p	21. bb	26. r
2. f	7. k	12. c	17. z	22. x	27. t
3. l	8. a	13. m	18. w	23. dd	28. aa
4. d	9. i	14. e	19. v	24. ee	29. y
5. n	10. o	15. j	20. u	25. cc	30. q

Key Term Matching II

1. d	5. h	9. j	13. g	17. n	21. u	25. v
2. l	6. k	10. c	14. t	18. x	22. s	
3. i	7. a	11. m	15. r	19. y	23. p	
4. f	8. e	12. b	16. w	20. q	24. o	

True/False Questions

1. T	6. T	11. T	16. T
2. T	7. T	12. T	17. F
3. F	8. T	13. T	18. F
4. F	9. F	14. T	19. T
5. T	10. F	15. F	20. T

Multiple-Choice Questions

1. D	6. C	11. D	16. B
2. A	7. A	12. A	17. B
3. D	8. D	13. C	18. C
4. B	9. C	14. D	19. C
5. A	10. B	15. C	20. D

CHAPTER 6
Development of Language and Symbol Use

Learning Objectives

Following the completion of the study of Chapter 6, you should be able to:

1. Name the distinguishing characteristics of **symbols** and of language as the preeminent symbol system.

2. Explain the components of language development, including **phonological development**, **semantic development**, **syntactic development**, **pragmatic development**, and **metalinguistic knowledge**.

3. Explain what is necessary for language learning, including both biological and social prerequisites, and why only humans achieve full-fledged language.

4. Describe the competencies in speech perception that are present in early infancy and the changes that occur in this aspect of language development before the end of the first year of life.

5. Describe the characteristics of babbling.

6. Discuss the role of the social context in the emergence of language production, including the ways in which it influences the infant's communicative competence.

7. Describe the characteristics of children's word production during the **holophrastic period** of language development.

8. Name multiple sources of support for learning new words, including examples of adult influences and children's own contributions to word learning.

9. Describe the developmental achievements that characterize children's acquisition of syntax.

10. Summarize the development of children's conversational skills during the preschool period.

11. Explain the major differences among three current theoretical perspectives on language development: **nativist views**, **interactionist views**, and **connectionist views**.

12. Present a piece of evidence that supports each of these views of language development and a major criticism of each view.

13. Explain the concept of **dual representation** and its significance in the development of symbolic proficiency.

14. Describe characteristics of children's early drawings.

15. Apply the material on language development to observations of children at different ages.

You Should Know:

Introduction

- what a symbol is and why the use of symbols is a crucial developmental task for humans.

Language Development (*summary on pg. 213 of text*)

Introduction
- which comes first, language comprehension or language production.

The Components of Language
- the multiple components involved in children's language development: phonological, semantic, syntactic, pragmatic, and metalinguistic.

What is Required for Language?
- to what extent animals other than humans can be credited with language and communicative systems.
- how the human brain is specialized for language, as well as how language capacity is localized in particular areas of the brain.
- the evidence for the existence of a critical period for language acquisition and how this has implications for foreign language training and the education of deaf children.
- the characteristics of infant-directed talk and why this type of talk is beneficial for infants' language acquisition.

Box 6.1 Applications: Two Languages are Better than One
- the developmental implications of bilingualism.
- what the controversy is in the United States regarding bilingualism in the classroom.

The Process of Language Acquisition
- how infants and adults perceive speech sounds and how these perceptions are influenced by nature and nurture.
- what research has been conducted to examine infants' perception of speech sounds, what this research has demonstrated about the similarities and differences between

the speech perceptions of infants and adults, and how infants' abilities to distinguish among speech sounds is associated with later language skills.

- what speech regularities are recognized by infants.

- what babbling is, how it develops, and how it and early communicative skills are influenced by nature and nurture.

- how infants' comprehension vocabulary and productive vocabulary develop at different rates and some of the difficulties infants encounter in each realm.

- the type of speech, types of words, and types of errors that are common in children's early speech.

- how adults influence children's word learning.

- how children actively contribute to their own word learning, including what types of assumptions they make about the meanings of words and what types of information they use to determine the meanings of words.

- how children's early sentences develop and what evidence exists for children's understanding of grammatical structure.

- how children's conversational skills develop and what parents do to influence the development of these skills.

Box 6.2 Theory in Action: Variability in Language Development

- what language development styles have been identified and how children who adopt different styles ultimately fare in the successful acquisition of language.

Box 6.3 A Closer Look: Language and Thought

- what research has suggested about the link between language and cognition.

Current Theoretical Issues in Language Development

- how nativists view language development and the cognitive abilities that support language.

- how researchers supporting an interactionist position view language development and the cognitive abilities that support language.

- how researchers supporting a connectionist position view language development and the cognitive abilities that support language.

- what support exists for each view, as well as what critics of each view argue.

Box 6.4 A Closer Look: "I Just Can't Talk Without My Hands": What Gestures Tell Us About Language

- how gestures are associated with language development for hearing and deaf children.

- how deaf children who invented sign languages can inform researchers' views of the innate nature of language and its components.

Nonlinguistic Symbols and Development (*summary on pg. 248 of text*)

Using Symbols as Information

- what is required in order for an individual to be able to use a symbolic artifact.
- how children's ability to achieve dual representation has been examined and what the research has demonstrated about the development of this ability.

Drawing

- how children's drawing ability develops and what this ability tells us about children's ability to use and create their own symbols.

Key Term Matching I: Definitions

Instructions: Match each key term with its definition.

Set A

KEY TERM

1.	_____	language comprehension	11.	_____	voice onset time
2.	_____	language production	12.	_____	object substitution
3.	_____	style	13.	_____	holophrastic period
4.	_____	phonological development	14.	_____	generativity
5.	_____	collective monologues	15.	_____	telegraphic speech
6.	_____	modularity hypothesis	16.	_____	semantic development
7.	_____	pragmatic development	17.	_____	narratives
8.	_____	dual representation	18.	_____	syntactic development
9.	_____	bilingualism	19.	_____	metalinguistic knowledge
10.	_____	categorical perception	20.	_____	intersubjectivity or joint attention

DEFINITION

a.   the length of time between when air passes through the lips and when the vocal cords start vibrating

b.   descriptions of past events that have the basic structure of a story

c.   the notion that we can put together an infinite number of sentences to express an infinite number of ideas using the finite set of words in our vocabulary

d.   the understanding of the properties and function of language

e.   the learning of the system for expressing meaning in a language

f.   the learning of the grammar of a language

g.   the stage in which infants use one word at a time

h.   the ability to use two languages

i.   the learning of the sound system of a language

j.   children's first sentences that are generally two-word utterances

k. understanding what others say or sign or write

l. the sharing of a common focus of attention by two or more people

m. the learning of knowledge about how language is used

n. the strategies young children enlist in beginning to speak

o. the perception of speech sounds as belonging to discrete categories

p. young children's talk with one another that often involves a series of unrelated statements

q. speaking (or signing or writing) to others

r. the argument that the human brain contains an innate, self-contained language component separate from other aspects of cognitive functioning

s. the notion that the use of a symbolic artifact requires mentally representing it both as a real object and as a symbol for something other than itself

t. A form of pretense in which an object is used as something other than itself

Set B

KEY TERM

21.	_____	symbols	30.	_____ overregularization
22.	_____	phonemes	31.	_____ morphemes
23.	_____	expressive style	32.	_____ infant-directed talk
24.	_____	syntax	33.	_____ overextension
25.	_____	fast mapping	34.	_____ critical period
26.	_____	wait-and-see style	35.	_____ prosody
27.	_____	pragmatic cues	36.	_____ syntactic bootstrapping
28.	_____	distributional properties	37.	_____ referential style
29.	_____	reference	38.	_____ universal grammar

DEFINITION

u.   a set of highly abstract, unconscious rules that are common to all languages

v.   a speech strategy that analyzes the speech stream into individual phonetic units

w.   the smallest units of meaning in a language

x.   the phenomenon that, in any language, certain sounds are more likely to appear together than are others

y.   the time during which language develops readily and after which language development becomes more difficult and less successful

z.   a special mode of talk that adults adopt when talking to babies and very young children

aa.   the characteristic rhythm, tempo, intonational patterns, etc. with which a language is spoken

bb.   the rules of a language that specify how words from different categories can be combined

cc.   the strategy of using the grammatical structure of whole sentences to determine the meaning of novel words

dd.   the use of a given word in a broader context than is appropriate

ee.   a speech strategy that gives more attention to the overall sound of language than to its phonetic elements

ff.   a speech strategy that results in children beginning to talk at a comparatively late age

gg.   the elementary units of meaningful sound that produce languages hh.   the process of learning a new word simply by noticing the contrastive use of it with a familiar word

ii.   speech errors in which children treat irregular forms of words as if they were regular

jj.   the association of words and meaning in language

kk.   aspects of the social context used for word learning

ll.   systems for representing thoughts, feelings and knowledge and communicating them to other people

Key Term Matching II: Applications, Examples, and More

Instructions: Match each key term with an application or example of the term.

Set A

KEY TERM

1. _____ language comprehension
2. _____ holophrastic period
3. _____ dual representation
4. _____ pragmatic development
5. _____ metalinguistic knowledge
6. _____ collective monologues
7. _____ categorical perception
8. _____ voice onset time
9. _____ intersubjectivity or joint attention

10. _____ language production
11. _____ object substitution
12. _____ telegraphic speech
13. _____ bilingualism
14. _____ narratives
15. _____ modularity hypothesis
16. _____ generativity
17. _____ style

APPLICATION OR EXAMPLE

a. these sentences omit nonessential elements, such as word endings and function words

b. even though a child can understand his parents' words, it is not until she speaks her own words that she is considered to be demonstrating this

c. with young infants, adults often establish this by talking about whatever the baby is looking at, but older infants are capable of following an adult's gaze

d. the learning of the cultural rule of referring to ships as female in the English language is considered part of this

e. this is supported by the fact that virtually all humans exposed to language successfully acquire it, whereas no other animals do

f. there appear to be cognitive benefits of this, and it does not appear to affect the course or rate of language development in either language

g. the finding that infants do this even for speech sounds they have never heard before demonstrates this is innate and is independent of experience

h. /b/ and /p/ differ only in this

i.   as a result of this, it is possible to form a sentence that that has never been uttered by any other person on earth

j.   a child who uses the word "nap-nap" to mean "I want to take a nap" is probably in this stage

k.   individual differences in this appear to have no long-term effects on children's ultimate language abilities

l.   A child who can understand his parents' words but cannot speak yet is demonstrating this

m.   this type of talk is common between preschoolers

n.   when children engage in this, they must ignore many of the real characteristics of the object so that it can serve the purpose of something else

o.   the understanding that all languages have words and that sentences are made up of words is part of this

p.   for a map, this involves both an understanding that it is a tangible piece of paper with lines and colors on it and an understanding that lines and colors on it represent roads, water, mountains, etc.

q.   five-year-olds' increased knowledge of the structure of stories helps them produce these

Set B

KEY TERM

18. _____   wait-and-see style
19. _____   phonemes
20. _____   morphemes
21. _____   expressive style
22. _____   critical period
23. _____   infant-directed talk
24. _____   prosody
25. _____   distributional properties
26. _____   syntactic bootstrapping

27. _____   referential style
28. _____   syntax
29. _____   symbols
30. _____   universal grammar
31. _____   fast mapping
32. _____   pragmatic cues
33. _____   reference
34. _____   overregularization
35. _____   overextension

APPLICATION OR EXAMPLE

r.   A child who uses the word "gooses" instead of "geese" is making this type of error

s.   newborns' preference for their mothers' language is due to their learning of this characteristic of the native language while in the womb

t.   a child who figures out the meaning of the novel word "basket" by her father's sentence "It's not in the bowl; it's in the basket" has used this

u.   even if one knew the meanings of all the words in the sentence "Big Bird gave Elmo the ball," one wouldn't be able to determine who was the giver and who was the receiver unless one understood the _____ of English

v.   the first utterances made by children with this style tend to be long "sentences" made up of hardly any recognizable words but uttered with perfect rhythm and intonation

w.   focus of attention and intentionality are examples of these

x.   in English, the word "cat" and the word "hat" differ in only one of these

y.   support for the existence of this comes from evidence that deaf children who had no linguistic input from adults spontaneously imposed a grammatical structure on their invented sign languages

z.   a child who thinks that the word "bird" represents the tall, leafy object that is inhabited by the small, black, singing object rather than representing the small, black, singing object itself, is having a problem with this aa.   the first utterances made by children with this style tend to be isolated, monosyllabic words

bb.   case studies of children deprived of communication, along with studies of brain organization in individuals who learned a second language at different ages, have provided evidence for the existence of this

cc.   children with this style are apparently listening very carefully because once they do speak, they tend to begin with a large number of clearly articulated words

dd.   a child's use of the word "kitty" for the squirrels she sees outside, even though she can tell the difference between her own house pet and the animals with the fluffy tails, is an example of this

ee.   in English, the word "chair" contains only one of these

ff.   this involves high pitch and extreme changes in intonation and is generally accompanied by exaggerated facial expressions

gg.   children who heard the sentence "The duck is kraddling the rabbit" and understood that "kraddling" involved only what the duck was doing to the rabbit (and not what the duck and rabbit were both doing) used this strategy to determine the meaning of the new word

hh.   pictures, numbers, models, and maps are examples of these

ii.   infants are sensitive to this, as was demonstrated by the finding that they listened longer to rarely-combined sounds than to commonly-combined sounds after being "taught" a set of novel "words"

True/False Questions

Instructions: Indicate whether each item is true or false.

_____   1.   The basic linguistic competence of five year olds whose native language is spoken is advanced in comparison to five year olds whose native language is manually signed.

_____   2.   The phonemes that distinguish meaning in any one language differ entirely from the phonemes that distinguish meaning in other languages.

_____   3.   Adults have considerable metalinguistic knowledge that young language learners do not have.

_____   4.   In a study of the English proficiency of Chinese and Korean immigrants to the United States, knowledge of some fine points of English grammar was associated with the age at which these individuals began learning English, but not with how long they had been in the United States.

_____   5.   Infants prefer to listen to infant-directed talk than to talk directed at adults.

_____   6.   Adults' inability to distinguish between phonemic contrasts that are not important in their native language but that are important in other languages partly accounts for why it is so difficult for adults to learn a second language.

_____   7.   Infants are unable to recognize the sound of their name until late in the first year.

_____   8.   Middle-class American mothers tend to label objects for their infants more than do Japanese mothers.

_____   9.   Toddlers who overextend words do so because they are unable to differentiate among the objects to which their words refer.

_____   10.   Fast mapping refers to toddlers' ability to quickly use a word they already know to refer to a new object for which they have no word.

_____   11.   Eighteen-month-olds are able to use both the emotional responses and the intentions of adults to infer the meanings of words.

_____   12.   Young children expect novel words in different grammatical categories (e.g., "daxing" versus "a dax") to have different types of meanings.

_____   13.   Young toddlers are able to differentiate between sentences with normal word order and sentences whose word order is scrambled before they are able to produce multiple-word sentences.

_____   14.   Early simple sentences tend not to follow the word order of children's native language.

_____   15.   Although parents do not often correct their young children's grammatical errors, they do frequently fill in the missing parts of their children's incomplete utterances.

_____ 16. Private speech of young children tends only to occur during solitary play and not in the company of other children.

_____ 17. Parents' scaffolding of toddlers' narratives is unassociated with the children's ability to produce narratives as preschoolers.

_____ 18. The modularity hypothesis states that the innate language module can function across many domains of cognitive functioning.

_____ 19. The fact that Genie's language development never progressed past the level of an average toddler is evidence for connectionist views of language acquisition.

_____ 20. Children begin to try to produce representational art at approximately the same age as they are able to successfully use a scale model of a room to find a hidden object in the room.

Multiple-Choice Questions

1. Learning which of the following is considered part of phonological development?
   A. how to produce the "r" sound
   B. the rules of negation
   C. how to take turns during conversations with others
   D. the contrast between the meanings of the words "table" and "desk"

2. Children's pragmatic development refers to their learning of the:
   A. meaning system and words of their language.
   B. cultural rules for how their language is used.
   C. rules for combining the words in their language.
   D. sound system of their language.

3. The critical period for language development applies to:
   A. learning of only the first language.
   B. learning of only languages that follow learning of the first language (i.e., second language, third language, etc.).
   C. learning of all languages, first and subsequent.
   D. none of the above, as there is no critical period for language development.

4. Which of the following is NOT a characteristic of infant-directed talk?
   A. extreme changes in intonation pattern
   B. extreme changes in volume
   C. slow and containing elongated pauses
   D. affectionate

5. Imagine a foreign language that contains two phonemes, /ʜ/ and /Ɛ/, which differ only in voice onset time (VOT). The VOT of /ʜ/ is much shorter (100 ms) than the VOT of /Ɛ/ (200 ms). Researchers are interested in how adult native speakers of this language perceive sounds that have all the same characteristics of /ʜ/ and /Ɛ/ except that they have a VOT that is *between* 100 and 200 ms. (Note that there are no phonemes in this language that fall between /ʜ/ and /Ɛ/.) Adult native speakers of the language listen to artificial speech sounds starting with a VOT of 100 ms and then with progressively longer VOTs until the sound /Ɛ/ is reached. How will these adults perceive the sound with a VOT of 130 ms?
   A. as a mixture of /ʜ/ and /Ɛ/
   B. as an unfamiliar phoneme
   C. as either /ʜ/ or /Ɛ/
   D. not as a speech sound

6. Young infants perceive speech sounds:
   A. continuously.
   B. in their native language categorically and those not in their native language continuously.
   C. categorically, perceiving *fewer* phonemic contrasts than do adults.
   D. categorically, perceiving *as many* phonemic contrasts as do adults.
   E. categorically, perceiving *more* phonemic contrasts than do adults.

7. Research on infants' sensitivity to the distributional properties of the speech they hear demonstrated that infants:
   A. are unable to recognize the syllables that are common in their native language.
   B. are sensitive to the recurrent patterns of syllables in their native language.
   C. cannot differentiate between all of the phonemes that sound different to adults.
   D. are unaware of the prosody of their native language.

8. The association of a word with its meaning is referred to as:
   A. orientation.
   B. intersubjectivity.
   C. reference.
   D. prosody.

9. "Mine" is an example of:
   A. nouncentric speech.
   B. overextension.
   C. holophrastic speech.
   D. telegraphic speech.
   E. pragmatism.

10. Which of the following children exhibits what language researchers refer to as an expressive or holistic style of language acquisition?
   A. Isaac, whose utterances have good intonation patterns, but few recognizable words
   B. Ricky, who only speaks with isolated, monosyllabic utterances
   C. Brenda, who is nearly silent, but who understands much of her parents' speech
   D. Abigail, who comprehends few of her parents' utterances

11. The study by Brown in which preschool children were shown hands kneading material in a container demonstrated that young children tend to interpret "a sib" to refer to:
   A. the material.
   B. the container.
   C. the act of kneading.
   D. any of the above.

12. Which of the following is likely to be included in telegraphic speech?
   A. action verbs
   B. auxiliary verbs
   C. verb tenses
   D. none of the above

13. Marcus' "rule and memory" model of children's grammar states that children make overregulation errors when they:
   A. are unable to remember a grammatical rule.
   B. make up their own grammar rules.
   C. forget the correct form of an irregular word and thus use the general rule by default.
   D. cannot figure out the appropriate grammar rule for a particular context.

14. Which of the following statements made by a two-year-old is a parent most likely to correct?
   A. "Where the baby is?"
   B. "Me want no shoes."
   C. "No read book."
   D. "Sky green."
   E. Parents would be equally likely to correct all of the above statements.

15. The term collective monologues is used to describe the common pattern of conversation among:
   A. infants.
   B. preschoolers.
   C. school-age children.
   D. adolescents.

16. Narratives primarily refer to descriptions of what type of events?
   A. present
   B. past
   C. future
   D. current

17. Which of the following views of language development supports the existence of universal grammar?
   A. nativist
   B. interactionist
   C. connectionist
   D. all of the above

18. Connectionist views of language development hold that the information needed to acquire language is:
A. held in the brain's language module.
B. learned in the social context in which language is used.
C. universal to all languages.
D. contained in the language itself.

19. To use a symbolic artifact, children must be able to represent the artifact as:
A. a real object only.
B. a symbol only.
C. neither a real object nor a symbol.
D. both a real object and a symbol.

20. To eliminate the need for dual representation, DeLoache and her colleagues used which of the following with 2½-year-olds?
A. a scale model of a large room
B. a map of a room
C. a shrinking machine
D. crayons and paper

Essay Questions

Instructions: Answer the following essay questions on a separate sheet of paper.

1. Imagine your new neighbors are recent immigrants from Brazil. They have an infant. Should your neighbors have any concern that hearing English will interfere with their baby's acquisition of their native language, including all of the sounds, rules, and meanings that differ from English?

2. Imagine a foreign language that contains two phonemes, /нь/ and /ξ/, that differ only in voice onset time. The voice onset time of /нь/ is much shorter (100 ms) than the voice onset time of /ξ/ (200 ms). Researchers are interested in how adult native speakers and infants from homes that speak this language perceive sounds that have all the same characteristics of /нь/ and /ξ/ except that they have a voice onset time between 100 and 200 ms. (Note that there are no phonemes in this language that fall between /нь/ and /ξ/, but other languages do use a phoneme, /ю/, with all of the same characteristics of /нь/ and /ξ/, except that it has a voice onset time of 145 ms.) Adult native speakers of the language listen to artificial speech sounds starting with /нь/ and then with progressively longer voice onset times until the sound /ξ/ is reached. How will native speakers of the language perceive the sounds with a voice onset time of between 100 and 200 ms? Why? How could infants' perceptions of the sounds with voice onset times of between 100 and 200 ms be examined? What is the likely result of this examination? Why?

3. Describe the characteristics of children's first words. Specifically, what types of words do children tend to say first? What types of words do they rarely say? Provide an example of each. In addition, what types of strategies do young children use to simplify words?

4. Choose an object that is important to you in some way (e.g., book, desk, hat) and discuss how you may have first learned this word as a young child. How might the adults around you have used this word when they were trying to teach you the word? What assumptions might you have made about what the novel word may have meant? What types of cues might have assisted you in learning the meaning of this word? Give specific examples to answer each question.

5. Discuss the concept of dual representation of a symbolic artifact and give an example of a symbolic artifact and its two possible representations. Why is the need to be able to represent a symbol in two ways necessary for the understanding of symbols?

Answer Key

Key Term Matching I

1. k	7. m	13. g	19. d	25. hh	31. w	37. v
2. q	8. s	14. c	20. l	26. ff	32. z	38. u
3. n	9. h	15. j	21. ll	27. kk	33. dd	
4. i	10. o	16. e	22. gg	28. x	34. y	
5. p	11. a	17. b	23. ee	29. jj	35. aa	
6. r	12. t	18. f	24. bb	30. ii	36. cc	

Key Term Matching II

1. l	7. g	13. f	19. x	25. ii	31. t
2. j	8. h	14. q	20. ee	26. gg	32. w
3. p	9. c	15. e	21. v	27. aa	33. z
4. d	10. b	16. i	22. bb	28. u	34. r
5. o	11. n	17. k	23. ff	29. hh	35. dd
6. m	12. a	18. cc	24. s	30. y	

True/False Questions

1. F	6. T	11. T	16. F
2. F	7. F	12. T	17. F
3. T	8. T	13. T	18. F
4. T	9. F	14. F	19. F
5. T	10. F	15. T	20. T

Multiple-Choice Questions

1. A	6. E	11. B	16. B
2. B	7. B	12. A	17. A
3. C	8. C	13. C	18. D
4. B	9. C	14. D	19. D
5. C	10. A	15. B	20. C

CHAPTER 7

Conceptual Development

Learning Objectives

Following the completion of the study of Chapter 7, you should be able to:

1. Recognize the general pattern of conceptual development apparent across all domains examined in this chapter: that understanding begins early in infancy but major improvements continue for many years thereafter.

2. Provide examples of the ways in which both nature and nurture play important roles in children's acquisition of concepts.

3. Explain **perceptual categorization** as a key element in infants' thinking.

4. Describe children's development of **category hierarchies**, with reference to the use of the **superordinate, basic,** and **subordinate levels**.

5. Explain what is meant by **naive psychology**, and describe the psychological constructs included in the naive psychology of children from infancy through age 5.

6. Give an example of a **false-belief problem** and predict a typical 3-year-old child's performance of this problem.

7. Describe the evidence in support of the existence of a **theory-of-mind module (TOMM)**.

8. Contrast the **pretend play** of typical 18-month-old and 3-year-old children.

9. Summarize children's development of the distinction between living and nonliving things.

10. Explain the role of **essentialism** in children's understanding of inheritance.

11. Contrast the nativist and empiricist explanations of children's acquistion of biological knowledge.

12. Identify the role of **egocentric representations**, landmarks, self-locomotion, and **dead reckoning** in developmental changes in the representation of space.

13. Describe the limitations in infants' and preschoolers' understanding of time.

14. Provide examples of the ways in which children's ability to identify causal relations expands with development.

15. Explain the major change that characterizes children's understanding of **numerical equality** from infancy to age 4.

16. Discuss two alternative explanations of the experimental evidence that infants understand simple arithmetic, incorporating the concept of **subitizing**.

17. Explain the five counting principles.

18. Observe examples of preschoolers' concepts of people, living things, space, time, causality and number in everyday interactions with children.

You Should Know:

Introduction

- what concepts are and why they are important.
- what factors are involved in conceptual development.
- how nativists and empiricists explain conceptual development.

Understanding Who or What (*summary on pg. 275 of text*)

Dividing Objects into Categories

- how children generally divide up things in the world and the form these categories take.
- what types of categories infants can form, how infants' category formation develops over the first year of life, and how this has been examined in research.
- how children's categorization improves beyond infancy and what contributes to this development.

Knowledge of Other People and Oneself

- what infants understand about other people.
- how children's understanding of others develops from ages two to five, including the components of children's theories of mind and the relations among the components.
- what errors preschoolers still make, how researchers have examined these errors, and what cross-cultural research has demonstrated about these errors.
- the controversy among the three explanations for how children acquire the ability to understand others, and how research with autistic children relates to this controversy.
- how children's pretend play develops and what its role is in the development of the understanding of others, according to Piaget, Vygotsky, and recent research.

Box 7.1: Theory in Action: Children with Autism

- what autism is and autistic children's typical pattern of understanding of people.

- how autistic children do on false-belief problems compared to typical children and to deaf and mentally retarded children.

Box 7.2: Theory in Action: Imaginary Companions

- how children who have imaginary companions are similar to and different from those who do not have imaginary companions.

- what purposes imaginary companions serve for children.

Knowledge of Living Things

- what young children do and do not understand about living things.

- when and how children begin to differentiate between living and nonliving things and among different types of living things, namely humans, other animals, and plants.

- how children's beliefs about inheritance, growth, illness, and healing develop.

- what controversy exists between nativists and empiricists regarding how children acquire biological knowledge, as well as what evidence researchers on different sides of the controversy use to support their positions.

Understanding Where, When, Why, and How Many (*summary on pg. 289 of text*)

Space

- how the brain is specialized for spatial thinking.

- how the ability to represent location relative to oneself develops in infancy, as well as what contributes to infants' sense of space independent of their own location.

- how the link between self-locomotion and spatial representation has been examined in infants and older children.

- how the ability to see influences spatial representation.

- how the abilities to represent location relative to multiple landmarks and relative to one's starting point develop.

- how the sociocultural context influences the development of spatial thinking.

Time

- how infants' and children's experience of time, including remembering the order of events and estimating the duration of events, develops.

- how children's ability to reason about longer time periods, in both the past and the future, develops.

- how children's ability to reason about time develops, including the constraints on this ability in younger children.

Causality

- how the nativists/empiricist debate extends to the development of causal reasoning.

- how infants are able to reason about physical causation, including how these understandings have been examined.

- how infants' understanding of causality influences their memory and imitation.

- how preschoolers' beliefs about causality develop and how these beliefs influence children's reactions to magic tricks.

Box 7.3: A Closer Look: Magical Thinking and Fantasy

- how preschoolers' understanding about causality is related to their magical thinking and fantasies.

- what magical beliefs are common in preschoolers, how children develop beyond their magical thinking.

Number

- how the nativists/empiricist debate extends to the concept of number.

- what young infants understand about number and how this understanding has been assessed.

- how infants' rudimentary ability to do arithmetic has been assessed, what these studies have demonstrated, and what controversy exists regarding the implications of this research.

- how children's understandings of number and arithmetic develop beyond infancy.

- how the ability to count develops, including what counting principles preschoolers appear to comprehend.

- how differences in language and sociocultural context influence the development of children's ability to count.

Key Term Matching I: Definitions

Instructions: Match each key term with its definition.

KEY TERM

1. _____ concepts

2. _____ category hierarchies

3. _____ perceptual categorization

4. _____ autism

5. _____ subordinate level

6. _____ basic level

7. _____ essentialism

8. _____ sociodramatic play

9. _____ numerical equality

10. _____ theory of mind

11. _____ false-belief problems

12. _____ subitizing

13. _____ superordinate level

14. _____ theory-of-mind module

15. _____ pretend play

16. _____ naive psychology

17. _____ egocentric representation

18. _____ dead reckoning

19. _____ object substitution

DEFINITION

a. tasks that test whether children understand that other people will act in accordance with their own beliefs, even when the child knows those beliefs to be wrong

b. the ability to continuously keep track of one's location relative to the starting point and thus be able to return directly to it

c. a hypothesized brain mechanism devoted to understanding other human beings

d. the most general level within a category hierarchy

e. a basic understanding of how the mind works and how it influences behavior

f. the middle level within a category hierarchy

g. a commonsense level of understanding of other people and oneself

h. the belief that living things have an essence inside them that makes them what they are

i. a form of pretense in which an object is used as something other than itself

j. make-believe activities in which children act as if they are in a different situation

k. general ideas or understandings that can be used to group together objects, events, etc., that are similar in some way

l.   a perceptual process by which adults and children can look at between one and three or four objects and almost immediately know how many objects are present

m.   a syndrome involving a number of intellectual and emotional difficulties, particularly in understanding and relating to other people

n.   the grouping together of objects with similar appearances

o.   the most specific level within a category hierarchy

p.   coding of spatial locations relative to one's own body, without regard to the surroundings

q.   activities in which children enact minidramas with other people

r.   categories that are related by set-subset relations

s.   the realization that all sets of N objects have something in common

Key Term Matching II: Applications, Examples, and More

Instructions: Match each key term with an application or example of the term.

KEY TERM

1. _____ theory-of-mind module
2. _____ category hierarchies
3. _____ subordinate level
4. _____ superordinate level
5. _____ false-belief problems
6. _____ basic level
7. _____ naive psychology
8. _____ object substitution
9. _____ autism
10. _____ pretend play

11. _____ perceptual categorization
12. _____ theory of mind
13. _____ concepts
14. _____ dead reckoning
15. _____ subitizing
16. _____ egocentric representation
17. _____ sociodramatic play
18. _____ numerical equality
19. _____ essentialism

APPLICATION OR EXAMPLE

a. these help us make sense of the world by simplifying it and allowing us to use our prior experience to interpret new situations

b. when children engage in this, they must ignore many of the real characteristics of the object so that it can serve the purpose of something else

c. this is a major component of infants' conceptual thinking, and often involves color or size

d. although some animals who forage for food and then must return home possess this ability, people are not very good at it

e. in the tool/screwdriver/flat-head screwdriver hierarchy, "flat-head screwdriver" is at this level

f. a child who uses a clean paint brush on the wall in a pretense of painting the wall is engaging in this broad term

g. infants tend to use this to locate an object, even when their own position has changed

h. the tool/screwdriver/flat-head screwdriver relation is an example of this

i. Wellman suggested that preschoolers' _____ includes the knowledge that beliefs often originate in perceptions

j.   children fail these tasks when they do not fully understand that others can have different beliefs than they themselves possess

k.   objects within this hierarchy level generally have many consistent characteristics and thus this level is often the first one learned by children

l.   even young infants appear to have a sense of this

m.   researchers who believe that children have a specialized _____ point to brain maturation over the first five years and to autistic children's difficulties with understanding other people as evidence

n.   An example of this is children playing "firefighter" with complete with imaginary hydrants, burning buildings, ladders, fire engines, and people to rescue.

o.   preschoolers' belief that cows have a certain "cowness" that they inherit from their parents reflects this way of thinking

p.   even infants have a simple theory of this type, probably as a result of their intense interest in people

q.   in the tool/screwdriver/flat-head screwdriver hierarchy, "tool" is at this level

r.   children, and even teenagers, who are affected by this syndrome find tasks examining understanding of other people's minds very difficult

s.   some researchers believe that young infants are doing this to "solve" arithmetic problems involving one to three objects

True/False Questions

Instructions: Indicate whether each item is true or false.

_____ 1. Empiricists believe that innate understanding of basic concepts plays a central role in development.

_____ 2. Infants use color as a cue to categorization at an earlier age than they use shape.

_____ 3. In the furniture/table/kitchen table hierarchy, kitchen table is at the basic level.

_____ 4. Children use what they know about basic categories to form subordinate and superordinate categories.

_____ 5. At the center of naive psychology are three concepts that we use of understand human behavior: desires, beliefs, and actions.

_____ 6. The understanding that people's desires influence their actions begins to develop toward the end of the second year of life.

_____ 7. The development of children's understanding of false beliefs varies widely by culture.

_____ 8. Some researchers have proposed that at the foundation of autistic children's limited involvement with the social world is a failure to understand other people.

_____ 9. Empiricists who emphasize social interactions as crucial to the development of psychological understanding cite evidence that preschoolers with older siblings do better on false-belief tasks than do those without them.

_____ 10. Pretend play and object substitution are types of sociodramatic play.

_____ 11. Recent research has supported Piaget's view that children's play simply reflects their general egocentrism and does not advance their developmental level.

_____ 12. Up to the age of 10, children often believe that animals and plants were created to serve specific purposes, in much the same way that people's creations are.

_____ 13. Although five year olds typically know a lot about the similarities among all living creatures, they often deny that humans are animals.

_____ 14. Preschoolers have a difficult time understanding that traits are passed from parents to their offspring.

_____ 15. Nativists propose that we are born with a "biology module" that helps children to learn quickly about living things.

_____ 16. From early in infancy, children need landmarks to enable them to code space.

_____   17.   Although visual experience in infancy appears to play an important role in spatial development, many blind people nonetheless develop impressive senses of space.

_____   18.   Preschoolers often count to estimate the passage of time, but they fail to understand the importance of counting at an even rate.

_____   19.   Many 9-year-olds and some adult still revert to magical explanations when confronted with a magic trick that was difficult to explain in physical terms.

_____   20.   Some researchers have proposed that infants' apparent ability to do arithmetic is actually due to their reliance on subitizing.

Multiple-Choice Questions

1. Categories that are related by set-subset relations are considered to be members of a:
   A. perception.
   B. concept.
   C. hierarchy.
   D. superordinate.

2. Which of the following is an example of a category hierarchy?
   A. furniture/inanimate objects/table
   B. people/Daddy/Mommy
   C. plants/daisies/living things
   D. animals/mammals/cows
   E. vehicles/cars/trains

3. Infants generally categorize objects as belonging to the same category when they have:
   A. a superordinate-subordinate relationship.
   B. similar appearances.
   C. causal relations.
   D. cross-class correspondences.

4. Which of the following groups constitute members of the same perceptual category?
   A. cat, dog, tiger
   B. bat, fist, tennis racquet
   C. clothing, pants, necklace
   D. knife, fork, pitcher

5. Which level of the kitchenware/cup/coffee mug hierarchy do children generally learn first?
   A. kitchenware
   B. cup
   C. coffee mug
   D. They learn all of the parts of the hierarchy simultaneously.

6. Ideas used to understand human behavior are referred to as:
   A. beliefs.
   B. naive psychological concepts.
   C. perceptions.
   D. intentional constructs.

7. Which of the following is NOT a category in Wellman's model of preschoolers' theory of mind?
   A. basic emotions
   B. action
   C. reaction
   D. moral rules
   E. beliefs

8. Ellie, a four-year-old, is told a story about a boy who loves ice cream from the ice cream truck. One summer day, the boy stands outside on the street curb. When asked why the boy is standing there, which of the following would be the response that Ellie would be LEAST likely to give?
   A. "The boy thinks the ice cream truck will come soon."
   B. "The boy wants ice cream."
   C. "The boy hears the ice cream truck."
   D. "He is waiting for his friend from across the street."

9. Marcy, a five-year-old, is shown a raisin box and then shown that it contains pennies. If asked what she had thought the box contained before being shown its true contents, Marcy will most likely say she had thought it contained:
   A. raisins.
   B. pennies.
   C. popcorn.
   D. quarters.

10. On false-belief problems, children who do not yet have a complete understanding of the relation between their own beliefs and others' beliefs:
   A. have difficulty understanding that other people could have false beliefs when they themselves know the truth.
   B. have difficulty understanding that other people could know the truth when they themselves have false beliefs.
   C. believe that others will not be convinced of the truth.
   D. believe that others will be difficult to fool.

11. Beginning at what age do a clear majority of children understand that plants are alive?
   A. 2 to 3 years old
   B. 4 to 6 years old
   C. 7 to 9 years old
   D. 10 to 12 years old

12. The finding that babies pay more attention to rabbits than they do to inanimate objects indicates that they:
   A. can distinguish between animals and inanimate objects.
   B. can differentiate between people and other animals.
   C. know that plants, animals, and humans all belong to the category of living things.
   D. demonstrate all of the above.

13. Which of the following is NOT a belief that is typical of preschoolers?
   A. Living things grow bigger because of something inside them.
   B. The properties of inanimate objects serve important functions for the object.
   C. Germs can make you sick, even if you don't know the germs are there.
   D. Physical characteristics tend to be passed on from parent to offspring.

14. The view that living things have something inside them that makes them what they are is referred to as:
   A. spiritualism.
   B. soulism.
   C. essentialism.
   D. the life-force principle.

15. An infant's ability to retrieve a hidden object when remaining in a single location is evidence for the infant's representation of space relative to:
   A. her own body.
   B. the hidden object.
   C. the external environment.
   D. the starting point.

16. Which of the following is a true statement about a five-year-old's ability to use landmarks to code the locations of hidden objects?
   A. They are UNABLE to use landmarks to code the locations of hidden objects.
   B. They are able to use landmarks to code the locations of hidden objects when there is only a SINGLE landmark and it is VERY CLOSE to the hidden object.
   C. They are able to use landmarks when there are MANY possible landmarks but when one landmark is located RIGHT NEXT TO the hidden object.
   D. They are able to use landmarks REGARDLESS of the number of landmarks and proximity to the hidden object.

17. Older infants possess the ability to:
    A. estimate the timing of past events.
    B. estimate the timing of future events.
    C. remember the order of events.
    D. estimate the duration of events.
    E. do all of the above.

18. Manny, a seven-month-old infant, is watching his big sister jump up and down. His sister repeatedly jumps twice and then pauses to wait for Manny's giggles. As she jumps, Manny's sister says, "jump, jump." After a minute or so of this, Manny becomes bored and stops giggling. His sister then changes the pattern to one jump and "jump." Manny responds to this change with renewed interest and giggling. Which of the following statements is true?
    A. Manny dishabituated to the "jump, jump" pattern.
    B. Manny habituated to the new "jump" pattern.
    C. Manny has a rudimentary understanding of numerical equality.
    D. Manny cannot discriminate between the number one and the number two.
    E. A, B, & C

19. Subitizing relies on:
    A. counting.
    B. guessing.
    C. perception.
    D. addition.

20. When asked the question, "Which is more X or Y?", three-year-olds can typically answer the question correctly when X and Y are numbers between 1 and:
    A. 2.
    B. 5.
    C. 10.
    D. 100.

Essay Questions

Instructions: Answer the following essay questions on a separate sheet of paper.

1. How does infants' attention to perceptual similarities among objects help them learn categories? Discuss the implications of this for the notion of the active child.

2. Describe the importance of developing categories for children's understanding of concepts and causal relations.

3. How do three-year-olds typically do at false-belief problems? How about five-year-olds? How could you try to teach a three-year-old to think more like a five-year-old about these problems?

4. Describe a typical preschooler's understanding of the differences and similarities among people, other animals, and plants.

5. Describe how the development of an understanding of time is continuous and how it is discontinuous.

Answer Key

Key Term Matching I

1. k	4. m	7. h	10. e	13. d	16. g	19. i
2. r	5. o	8. q	11. a	14. c	17. p
3. n	6. f	9. s	12. l	15. j	18. b

Key Term Matching II

1. m	4. q	7. p	10. f	13. a	16. g	19. o
2. h	5. j	8. b	11. c	14. d	17. n
3. e	6. k	9. r	12. i	15. s	18. l

True/False Questions

1. F	6. F	11. F	16. F
2. T	7. F	12. T	17. T
3. F	8. T	13. T	18. T
4. T	9. T	14. F	19. T
5. T	10. F	15. T	20. T

Multiple-Choice Questions

1. C	6. B	11. C	16. D
2. D	7. D	12. A	17. C
3. B	8. D	13. B	18. C
4. A	9. A	14. C	19. C
5. B	10. A	15. A	20. B

CHAPTER 8

Intelligence and Academic Achievement

Learning Objectives

Following the completion of the study of Chapter 8, you should be able to:

1. Describe the contributions of Alfred Binet and his colleague Théophile Simon to intelligence testing.

2. Compare definitions of intelligence that view intelligence as one thing, a few things, or many things, incorporating the concepts of *g*, **fluid intelligence, crystallized intelligence**, **primary mental abilities**, and the **three-stratum theory of intelligence**.

3. Name the most widely used intelligence test for children, lists its two major sections and give an example of the subtests included under each major section.

4. Explain what IQ is and what it does and does not predict.

5. Provide specific examples of the ways in which a child's own characteristics, including genetic factors, influence the development of intelligence.

6. Discuss the components of the child's immediate environment, including experiences in the family and with schooling, that contribute significantly to the development of intelligence.

7. Examine the bases for group differences in intelligence.

8. Identify risk factors associated with the failure to reach one's intellectual potential and discuss practices that should be included in educational intervention programs for children at risk.

9. Explain the differences among alternative views on intelligence and the perspectives that underlie IQ testing. Compare Gardner's **multiple intelligence theory** and Sternberg's **theory of successful intelligence**.

10. Describe the five stages of reading development. Describe the processes of prereading skills, word identification, and comprehension that contribute to reading development.

11. Discuss the way that children use a **strategy-choice process** to choose adaptively between **phonological recoding** and **visually based retrieval** in reading.

12. Explain the role of **phonological processing** in **dyslexia**.

13. Give an example of how a student might form a **mental model** in reading comprehension.

14. Discuss the ways in which basic capacities, strategies, metacognitive processes, and content knowledge influence the development of skill in writing.

15. Provide examples of children's use of overt strategies in learning arithmetic.

16. Explain the differences between groups of good students, not-so-good students, and perfectionists.

17. Discuss the significance of **mathematical equality** in learning arithmetic.

18. Based on the material in the text, generate recommendations for components of programs designed to develop and improve the mathematics skills of children who are likely to experience difficulties in learning math.

You Should Know:

Introduction

- the historical background of intelligence testing.
- the implications of Binet's theory of intelligence for other aspects of psychology.

What Is Intelligence? (*summary on pg. 297 of text*)

Intelligence as a Single Trait

- what *g* is hypothesized to be and what evidence supports its existence.

Intelligence as a Few Basic Abilities

- what crystallized and fluid intelligence are hypothesized to be and what evidence exists to support their distinction.
- how Thurstone viewed intelligence and what evidence exists to support his view.

Intelligence as Multiple Processes

- how information-processing theorists conceive of intelligence.
- the benefits and costs of viewing intelligence as many things versus a few things versus one thing.

A Proposed Resolution

- how John Carroll proposed to resolve the different perspectives on intelligence.

Measuring Intelligence (*summary on pg. 301 of text*)

The Contents of Intelligence Tests
- how the content of intelligence tests varies with the age of the children being tested and why this is the case.
- what the most widely used intelligence test for children six years of age and older tests and how the sections are related to fluid and crystallized intelligence.

The Intelligence Quotient (IQ)
- what an individual's intelligence quotient tells us about his or her intelligence.
- the extent to which individuals' IQ scores are consistent over time and what influences the degree of consistency.
- what level of success researchers have had at measuring infants' intelligence.

Box 8.1: Individual Differences: Gifted Children
- the two different types of gifted children and the common characteristics of the two types of gifted children.
- the factors involved in whether gifted children make outstanding contributions as adults.

IQ Scores as Predictors of Important Outcomes (*summary on pg. 302 of text*)

- how IQ is associated with long-term outcomes, as well as how other factors play a role.

Genes, Environment, and the Development of Intelligence (*summary on pg. 313 of text*)

Qualities of the Child
- the extent to which differences among individuals in IQ can be attributed to genetic differences, as well as how the genetic contribution to intelligence changes with development.
- how the three types of gene-environment effects proposed by Sandra Scarr contribute to individual differences in intelligence.

Influence of the Immediate Environment
- how aspects of the family environment that may influence intelligence have been assessed and what association has been found between family environment and intelligence.

- how shared and nonshared family environments are associated with children's IQ and how the influence of the shared environment can differ by socioeconomic status and race.
- how school attendance is related to IQ, what types of evidence have pointed to this association, and the social policy implications of this finding.

Influence of Society
- what the Flynn Effect is and what explanation exists for it.
- how poverty is associated with IQ and what factors account for this association.
- what it means to be a resilient child and how resilient children differ from their peers.
- how race is associated with IQ, how these differences are influenced by differences in social-class background, and what facts we need to be aware of when drawing conclusions about these differences.
- what risk factors are associated with IQ scores and the implications of this research for demonstrating the importance of the environment in the development of intelligence.
- what interventions have attempted to improve children's IQs, as well as what factors influenced whether these interventions were successful.

Box 8.2: Applications: A Highly Successful Early Intervention: The Carolina Abecedarian Project
- the features of the Carolina Abecedarian Project, the extent to which the project was successful, and the implications of the project's success for the development of other intervention programs.

Alternative Perspectives on Intelligence (*summary on pg. 315 of text*)

- what Gardner and Sternberg believe is missing from traditional tests of intelligence and how they conceive of intelligence.
- what evidence exists to support the views of contemporary theorists and how we can reconcile these contemporary views with traditional conceptions of intelligence.

Acquisition of Academic Skills (*summary on pg. 329 of text*)

Reading
- how children's ability to read develops from birth through adolescence.
- how children develop phonemic awareness and how phonemic awareness in preschool is associated with later reading achievement.
- what strategies children use to identify written words and how they choose between strategies.

- what is involved in reading comprehension, how it develops, and what factors influence children's reading comprehension ability.

Box 8.3: Individual Differences: Dyslexia

- what dyslexia is and what weakness accounts for most cases of dyslexia.
- what types of training can help children with dyslexia.

Writing

- what parallels exist between the development of reading and the development of writing.
- what skills are involved in writing and what types of strategies help children become better writers.

Mathematics

- what strategies children use to solve arithmetic problems, how children choose among these strategies, and how different types of children choose differently.
- how shallow understanding of mathematical concepts can lead to difficulty with novel problems, as well as what behaviors indicate that a child is ready to learn from instruction.
- how sociocultural factors influence children's mathematical abilities.

Box 8.4: Applications: Mathematical Disabilities

- what difficulties children with mathematical disabilities encounter and what causes their difficulties.
- how interventions have attempted to help these children and the extent to which these programs have succeeded.

Key Term Matching I: Definitions

Instructions: Match each key term with its definition.

Set A

KEY TERM

1. _____ *g* (general intelligence)
2. _____ strategy-choice process
3. _____ fluid intelligence
4. _____ primary mental abilities
5. _____ mental model
6. _____ phonemic awareness
7. _____ dyslexia
8. _____ visually based retrieval
9. _____ crystallized intelligence
10. _____ phonological recoding
11. _____ IQ
12. _____ theory of successful intelligence

DEFINITION

a.   proceeding directly from the visual form of the word to its meaning

b.   Sternberg's theory of intelligence that views intelligence as the ability to do well in life

c.   ability to think on the spot to solve novel problems

d.   the inability to read well despite being of normal intelligence

e.   a summary measure used to indicate an individual's intelligence relative to others of the same age

f.   procedure for selecting among alternative ways of solving problems

g.   the ability to translate letters into sounds and to blend sounds into words

h.   the part of intelligence that is common to all intellectual tasks

i.   the ability to identify component sounds within spoken words

j.   factual knowledge about the world

k.   seven abilities suggested by Thurstone to be crucial to intelligence

l.   processes used to represent a situation or sequence of events

Set B

KEY TERM

13. _____ three-stratum theory of intelligence

14. _____ multiple intelligence theory

15. _____ normal distribution

16. _____ comprehension monitoring

17. _____ mathematical equality

18. _____ Wechsler Intelligence Scale for Children

19. _____ gesture-speech mismatches

20. _____ phonological processing

21. _____ standard deviation

22. _____ Project Rightstart

23. _____ Carolina Abecedarian Project

DEFINITION

m. a curriculum designed to prepare kindergarteners from low-income backgrounds for elementary school mathematics

n. a widely-used instrument designed to assess the intelligence of children ages six and older

o. the ability to discriminate and remember sounds within words

p. a pattern of data in which scores fall symmetrically around a mean value, with most scores falling close to the mean and few scores falling far from the mean

q. a comprehensive and successful enrichment program for children from low-income families

r. Gardner's theory of intelligence that claims that people possess eight intelligences

s. a measure of the variability of scores within a distribution

t. a phenomenon in which hand movements convey different ideas than verbal statements

u. the process of keeping track of one's understanding of material as it is read

v. Carroll's model of intelligence that proposes a hierarchy in which *g* is at the top and many specific processes are at the bottom

w. the idea that the values on the two sides of an equal sign must balance

Key Term Matching II: Applications, Examples, and More

Instructions: Match each key term with an application or example of the term.

Set A

KEY TERM

1. _____ mental model

2. _____ phonemic awareness

3. _____ strategy-choice process

4. _____ primary mental abilities

5. _____ IQ

6. _____ crystallized intelligence

7. _____ phonological recoding

8. _____ visually based retrieval

9. _____ fluid intelligence

10. _____ g (general intelligence)

11. _____ dyslexia

12. _____ multiple intelligence theory

APPLICATION OR EXAMPLE

a. high levels of this are associated with performance in school, with cognitive processing characteristics such as information-processing speed, and with high levels of knowledge of subjects not studied in school

b. this process is used to read words without sounding them out

c. evidence of child prodigies who were exceptional in only one particular area and of brain damage patients who had only one particular deficit support Gardner's _____

d. these include reasoning, perceptual speed, and spatial visualization

e. children with this syndrome read much less well than would be predicted by their IQ

f. a child who has developed this understands that there are three distinct sounds in "bat"

g. this tends to peak in early adulthood and slowly decline thereafter

h. examples of this include knowledge of state capitals, past presidents of the U.S., and arithmetic facts

i. a score of 100 on this measure indicates that an individual is of average intelligence for his or her age group

j. reading comprehension involves forming a _____ of the situation or idea being depicted in the text and continuously updating it

k.   in reading, children use this to determine whether to sound out a word or retrieve it from memory

l.   a child who has developed this ability can sound out the written word "bat"

Set B

KEY TERM

13. _____ three-stratum theory of intelligence

14. _____ Project Rightstart

15. _____ normal distribution

16. _____ phonological processing

17. _____ theory of successful intelligence

18. _____ gesture-speech mismatches

19. _____ Wechsler Intelligence Scale for Children

20. _____ standard deviation

21. _____ comprehension monitoring

22. _____ Carolina Abecedarian Project

APPLICATION OR EXAMPLE

m. a child who does not engage in this will not realize that he is not able to understand what is happening in a story he is reading and thus will not go back and reread a difficult passage

n. this program attempts to give children from low-income families experiences common in middle-class families that teach mathematical lessons, such as playing board games

o. this demonstrated the importance of beginning intervention programs early and continuing them for an extended period of time

p. most children with dyslexia are poor at reading because of a general weakness at this

q. this includes a Verbal section and a Performance section

r. according to this, people who can build on their strengths, compensate for their weaknesses, and select environments in which they can succeed are considered of high intelligence

s. children who show these when they explain their incorrect answer are more likely to benefit from instruction than other children

t. in a normal distribution, 68% of scores fall within one _____ of the mean

u. this may resolve the controversy over whether intelligence is a single entity or multiple processes

v. the fact that intelligence scores (along with many, many other variables such as height and weight) fall into this pattern allows for the assignment of IQ scores that are based on mean and standard deviation

True/False Questions

Instructions: Indicate whether each item is true or false.

_____ 1. Fluid intelligence is closely related to speed of processing and ability to control attention.

_____ 2. The three-stratum theory of intelligence includes general intelligence, fluid intelligence, and crystallized intelligence.

_____ 3. Intelligence tests are a direct measure of capacity to learn.

_____ 4. The WISC includes sections testing digit span, block design, and mazes.

_____ 5. IQ scores reflect both the mean for the test and its standard deviation.

_____ 6. A person's IQ scores at two different ages are generally identical.

_____ 7. Active effects of the genotype involve children's choices of environments that they enjoy.

_____ 8. The HOME measures the physical environment in which the child lives, but it does not assess aspects of the nonshared environment.

_____ 9. Among children from impoverished backgrounds, the shared environment accounts for more of the variance in IQ than genetics does.

_____ 10. Age is a more important predictor of IQ than is years of schooling.

_____ 11. The Flynn Effect appears to be explained by the increase in IQ scores among the smartest individuals.

_____ 12. Poor families in the United States are much poorer than their counterparts in many other developed nations.

_____ 13. There is far more variability in IQ among racial groups than there is within racial groups.

_____ 14. The number of risk factors in a four-year-old child's environment is highly correlated with the child's IQ at age 13.

_____ 15. Participation in Head Start does not appear to have long-lasting effects on IQ and achievement test scores.

_____ 16. Children tend to learn how to read simple material some time before they acquire phonological recoding skills.

_____ 17. Teaching phonemic awareness to four- and five-year-old children causes them to be better readers for at least several years after the training.

_____ 18. The strategy-choice process operates under the assumption that accuracy is more important than speed.

_____   19.   Children as young as three years old have an expectation that meaning should be reflected in print.

_____   20.   Children who demonstrate a mismatch between their gestures and their verbal statements when explaining their incorrect answers on mathematical problems tend to have particular difficulty with subsequent learning.

Multiple-Choice Questions

1. Positive correlations among dissimilar intellectual tasks has led to the hypothesis of the existence of:
   A. crystallized intelligence.
   B. general intelligence.
   C. fluid intelligence.
   D. three-stratum intelligence.

2. Fluid intelligence includes which of the following?
   A. knowledge of state birds
   B. ability to define words
   C. ability to draw inferences
   D. knowledge of grammatical rules
   E. all of the above

3. The three levels, from the top of the hierarchy to the bottom, as proposed by the three-stratum theory of intelligence are:
   A. "*g*", moderately general abilities, specific processes
   B. specific processes, "*g*", moderately general abilities
   C. "*g*", moderately general abilities, primary mental abilities
   D. primary mental abilities, moderately general abilities, specific processes

4. The Verbal Section of the WISC primarily measures:
   A. general intelligence.
   B. fluid intelligence.
   C. performance intelligence.
   D. crystallized intelligence.

5. IQ refers to:
   A. intelligence quarterly.
   B. individuality quotient.
   C. intelligence quotient.
   D. none of the above.

6. The correlation between IQ at one age and IQ at another age is LOWEST for which of the following pairs of ages?
   A. 6 years and 7 years
   B. 6 years and 8 years
   C. 7 years and 8 years
   D. 7 years and 9 years
   E. A and C are equally low.
   F. B and D are equally low.

7. Which of the following is an example of a passive effect of the genotype on scientific understanding?
   A. Sally joins the science club at school.
   B. Gabriel loves the science museum, so his parents take him often.
   C. Charlotte is curious about scientific phenomenon, so her parents explain many to her.
   D. Blake's parents love to read about science, so they have many science books and magazines in their home.

8. Which type of variation seems to have the greatest impact on the development of intelligence?
   A. shared environment
   B. within-family differences
   C. between-family differences
   D. cultural characteristics

9. Which of the following provides evidence for the conclusion that attending school increases IQ?
   A. Children's IQs increase with age.
   B. Children's IQs decrease over the summer vacation.
   C. Older children have slightly higher IQs than younger children in the same grade.
   D. All of the above provide evidence for this conclusion.

10. The gap between wealthy families and families living in poverty is greatest in which of the following countries?
    A. Canada
    B. Germany
    C. United States
    D. Great Britain

11. The Flynn Effect describes the finding that, over the past several generations, average IQ scores have:
  A. decreased.
  B. increased.
  C. become more varied.
  D. remained nearly exactly the same.

12. Which of the following is a risk factor on Sameroff's Environmental Risk Scale?
  A. African-American family
  B. maternal employment
  C. paternal education
  D. involvement of extended family

13. Project Head Start focuses on which facets of children's development?
  A. intellectual growth only
  B. physical growth only
  C. social and emotional growth only
  D. intellectual and physical growth only
  E. intellectual, physical, social, and emotional growth

14. Who is the founder of the theory of successful intelligence?
  A. Stanford
  B. Scarr
  C. Wechsler
  D. Sternberg

15. The ability to identify the component sounds within spoken words is referred to as:
  A. phonological recoding skills.
  B. strategy-choice process.
  C. mental model production.
  D. phonemic awareness.

16. The strategy-choice process involves choosing:
  A. among equally good strategies.
  B. the process that is least likely to result in an error.
  C. the strategy that will be fastest.
  D. the fastest approach that will be most likely to be correct.

17. Which of the following has the largest impact on reading comprehension?
   A. children's writing ability
   B. content knowledge
   C. strategy-choice process
   D. phonological awareness

18. When asked what 3 + 3 equals, Chelsea immediately answers, "6." Chelsea has most likely used which of the following arithmetic strategies?
   A. decomposition
   B. retrieval
   C. counting from 1
   D. counting from the larger addend

Essay Questions

Instructions: Answer the following essay questions on a separate sheet of paper.

1. What do you think intelligence is? How should we define it? How should we test it?

2. Describe the three types of processes that Sandra Scarr has proposed to account for gene-environment relations. Give an example of each.

3. Describe the characteristics of the average early intervention project aimed at poor children's intellectual development. Were these interventions successful? In what ways were they unsuccessful? How is the Carolina Abecedarian Project different from these intervention programs? Do these differences matter in terms of the effects of this intervention?

4. Describe how traditional theories of intelligence differ from more recent alternative perspectives by Gardner and Sternberg. What are the advantages and disadvantages of the traditional theories? What are the advantages and disadvantages of the alternative theories?

5. What advice would you give to parents of preschoolers about what they can do to best prepare their children for becoming good readers?

Answer Key

Key Term Matching I

1. h	5. l	9. j	13. v	17. w	21. s
2. f	6. i	10. g	14. r	18. n	22. m
3. c	7. d	11. e	15. p	19. t	23. q
4. k	8. a	12. b	16. u	20. o	

Key Term Matching II

1. j	5. i	9. g	13. u	17. r	21. m
2. f	6. h	10. a	14. n	18. s	22. o
3. k	7. l	11. e	15. v	19. q	
4. d	8. b	12. c	16. p	20. t	

True/False Questions

1. F	6. F	11. F	16. F
2. F	7. T	12. T	17. T
3. F	8. F	13. F	18. F
4. T	9. T	14. T	19. T
5. T	10. F	15. T	20. F

Multiple-Choice Questions

1. B	6. B	11. B	16. D
2. C	7. D	12. A	17. B
3. A	8. B	13. E	18. B
4. D	9. B	14. D	
5. C	10. C	15. D	

CHAPTER 9
Theories of Social Development

Learning Objectives

Following the completion of the study of Chapter 9, you should be able to:

1. Explain the function of three personality structures proposed by Freud—the **id**, the **ego**, and the **superego.**

2. Identify the **erogenous zone** that is central to each of Freud's five stages of psychosexual development.

3. Discuss the developmental issues that must be resolved in each of the first five stages of Erikson's theory of psychosocial development.

4. Describe the similarities and differences between Freud's and Erikson's psychoanalytic theories.

5. Explain the use of learning principles in **systematic desensitization** and **behavior modification**.

6. Explore the implications of the differences between Watson's behaviorism and Skinner's operant conditioning for the acquisition of behavior.

7. Discuss the role of **vicarious reinforcement** and **reciprocal determinism** in social learning theory.

8. With reference to the social cognitive theories of Selman and Dodge, provide an example of **self-socialization in social development**.

9. Discuss the importance of **attributions** in social cognitive theories.

10. Explain the role of evolution in ethological and evolutionary theories.

11. Give an example of an influence within each of the nested structures— **microsystem, mesosystem, exosystem, macrosystem, and chronosystem**—that constitute the environment in Bronfenbrenner's bioecological model.

12. Define ADHD and identify factors that contribute to this syndrome.

13. Evaluate the present status of each of the major categories of theories of social development, as presented in this chapter.

Psychoanalytic Theories (*summary on pg. 342 of text*)

View of Children's Nature
- what factors Freud and Erikson viewed as driving development.

Central Developmental Issues
- where Freud's and Erikson's theories stand on the issues of continuity/discontinuity and nature/nurture and the extent to which they focus on individual differences.

Freud's Theory of Psychosexual Development
- what Freud believed changed with development and how he conceived of each stage of development, including how the three personality structures develop during this time.
- how Freud believed healthy development culminated.

Erikson's Theory of Psychosocial Development
- what characterized each of the first five stages of Erikson's theory.
- what healthy development and unhealthy development look like at each stage and what parents can do to help children resolve each conflict successfully.
- how Freud's and Erikson's theories were similar and how they were different.

Current Perspectives
- what lasting contributions Freud's and Erikson's theories made on the field of developmental psychology.
- how Freud's and Erikson's theories are viewed by contemporary developmentalists and why this is the case.

Learning Theories (*summary on pg. 349 of text*)

View of Children's Nature
- what learning theorists emphasize as important in the shaping of personality and social behavior, including how traditional learning theorists and more contemporary learning theorists differ.

Central Developmental Issues
- where learning theorists stand on the issue of continuity/discontinuity and the extent to which they focus on specific mechanisms of change.

Watson's Behaviorism
- how Watson viewed development, the role of the "mind," and the role of parents in development.
- how Watson's experiences with Little Albert and two-year-old Peter have had a lasting impact on the treatment of fears and phobias.

Skinner's Operant Conditioning
- how Skinner's theory of operant conditioning has informed current thinking about child development and the ways that parents reinforce behavior unintentionally.
- how Skinner's theory led to the use of behavior modification.

Social Learning Theory
- how social learning theory is similar to and differs from traditional learning theories.
- the role of observational learning in development.
- how Bandura proposed individuals play an active role in their own development and the role of perceived self-efficacy.

Box 9.1: A Closer Look: Bandura and Bobo
- how Bandura examined the roles of observational learning and vicarious reinforcement in learning and what this research demonstrated.

Current Perspectives
- what lasting contributions learning theories made on the field of developmental psychology and what their major weaknesses are.

Theories of Social Cognition (*summary on pg. 354 of text*)

Introduction
- what role cognitive development plays in theories of social cognition.

View of Children's Nature
- what is viewed by social cognitive theorists as shaping development.

Central Developmental Issues
- what role the active child and individual differences themes play in theories of social cognition and where the theories stand on the continuity/discontinuity issue.

Selman's Stage Theory of Role Taking
- why role taking was considered by Selman to be important.

- how children's role taking ability progresses through four stages and how these stages are associated with stages of cognitive development.

Dodge's Information-Processing Theory of Social Problem Solving
- what role cognitive processes are viewed to play in social behavior, according to the information-processing approach.
- what steps children proceed through when faced with a social problem.
- how children with a hostile attributional bias differ from other children in these processes and how this influences peer behavior and children's beliefs.

Dweck's Theory of Self-Attributions and Academic Achievement
- the different patterns exhibited by children when they are faced with failure at a task.
- how children's theories of intelligence and success are associated with these differences in children's responses to failure.
- how parents may influence children's orientation toward learning and what can be done to help children who exhibit a helpless pattern.

Current Perspectives
- what lasting contributions social cognitive theories have made on the field of developmental psychology and what their major weakness is.

Ecological Theories of Development *(summary on pg. 370 of text)*

View of Children's Nature
- how ecological theories view children and the role of context and evolution in development.

Central Developmental Issues
- the extent to which ecological theories focus on the interaction of nature and nurture, the importance of the sociocultural context, and the role children play in their own development.

Ethological and Evolutionary Theories
- what ethology is and how an ethological approach has been applied to developmental issues, including imprinting and the play preferences of males and females.
- what the central premise of evolutionary psychology is and the types of issues on which evolutionary psychologists typically focus.

The Bioecological Model

- how Bronfenbrenner conceptualized the environment, the role of each environmental level in children's development, and the interaction between various contexts and contextual levels.

- what is meant by child maltreatment and what types of maltreatment exist.

- the factors related to child maltreatment at different levels of the bioecological model, how child maltreatment is associated with children's development, and what interventions may be effective in reducing the likelihood of maltreatment.

- the extent to which children are exposed to media and how exposure to media is thought to be associated with physical inactivity and obesity, social isolation, and social inequities.

- what concerns exist about children's exposure to media violence and pornography and the ways in which media violence exerts its influence on children.

- the ways in which socioeconomic status influences the development of children at every level of the bioecological model.

- the ways in which affluence can be costly to children's development.

Box 9.2: Theory in Action: Attention-Deficit Hyperactivity Disorder

- what symptoms are associated with ADHD, and how ADHD development.

- how biology and environmental factors in various levels of the bioecological model play a role in ADHD and its treatment.

Box 9.3: Applications: Preventing Child Maltreatment

Current Perspectives

- what contributions these theories have made on the field of developmental psychology and what criticisms of these theories have been made.

Key Term Matching I: Definitions

Instructions: Match each key term with its definition.

Set A

KEY TERM

1.	_____	vicarious reinforcement	10. _____	reciprocal determinism
2.	_____	erogenous zones	11. _____	self-socialization
3.	_____	systematic desensitization	12. _____	ADHD
4.	_____	child maltreatment	13. _____	behavior modification
5.	_____	superego	14. _____	Electra complex
6.	_____	internalization	15. _____	perceived self-efficacy
7.	_____	id	16. _____	ego
8.	_____	Oedipus complex	17. _____	imprinting
9.	_____	psychic energy		

DEFINITION

a.   Bandura's concept that children are affected by aspects of their environment, but that they also influence their environment

b.   the notion that children actively shape their own development

c.   a syndrome that involves difficulty sustaining attention

d.   in Freud's theory, the personality structure that is the rational, logical, problem-solving component of personality

e.   a process in which newborn birds and mammals of some species become attached to their mother at first sight and follow her everywhere

f.   in Freud's theory, the most primitive personality structure; it is unconscious and operates with the goal of seeking pleasure

g.   a form of therapy based on classical conditioning, in which positive responses are gradually conditioned to stimuli that initially elicit a highly negative response

h.   a form of therapy based on operant conditioning, in which reinforcement contingencies are changed to encourage more adaptive behavior

i.   observing another person receive a reward or punishment

j.   Freud's term for the biologically based instinctual drives that energize behavior, thoughts, and feelings

k.   in Freud's theory, areas of the body that are physically sensitive

l.   in Freud's theory, the personality structure that consists of internalized moral standards

m.   Freud's term for the psychosexual conflict experienced by boys, in which they have a form of sexual desire for their mothers and fear retaliation from their fathers

n.   intentional abuse or neglect that endangers anyone under the age of 18

o.   the process of adopting one's parents rules and standards as one's own

p.   a person's beliefs about how effectively he or she can control his or her own behavior, thoughts, and emotions in order to achieve a desired goal

q.   Freud's term for the psychosexual conflict experienced by girls, in which they have a erotic feelings toward their fathers and see their mothers as rivals

Set B

KEY TERM

18.	_____	hostile attributional bias	27.	_____	parental-investment theory
19.	_____	anal stage	28.	_____	macrosystem
20.	_____	incremental theory	29.	_____	helpless orientation
21.	_____	latency period	30.	_____	ethology
22.	_____	genital stage	31.	_____	exosystem
23.	_____	role taking	32.	_____	microsystem
24.	_____	oral stage	33.	_____	phallic stage
25.	_____	entity theory	34.	_____	mastery orientation
26.	_____	mesosystem	35.	_____	chronosystem

DEFINITION

r.   in bioecological theory, the larger cultural and social context within which all other systems are embedded

s.   the ability to adopt the perspective of another person

t.   the third stage of Freud's theory, in which sexual pleasure is focused on the genitalia

u.   a response to failure in which individuals try harder to succeed at the task and do not feel negatively about themselves

v.   the study of behavior within an evolutionary context

w.   the second stage of Freud's theory, in which the primary source of pleasure comes from defecation

x.   in Dodge's theory, the expectation that others' ambiguous behaviors originate from a hostile intent

y.   in bioecological theory, the immediate environment in which an individual directly participates

z.   in bioecological theory, historical circumstances that change over time and influence the other systems

aa.   in bioecological theory, the settings that influence a child's development but that a child does not directly experience bb.   the first stage of Freud's theory, in which the primary source of gratification is sucking and eating

cc.   in bioecological theory, the interconnections among aspects of the immediate environment

dd.   the fifth and final stage of Freud's theory, in which sexual maturation is complete and sexual intercourse becomes a major goal

ee.   a theory that stresses the evolutionary basis of parental behavior, including the enormous amounts of time, energy, and resources parents devote to their children

ff.   the belief that that a person's level of intelligence is fixed and unchangeable

gg.   the belief that intelligence is not fixed and can grow as a function of experience

hh.   the fourth stage of Freud's theory, in which sexual energy gets channeled into socially acceptable activities

ii.   a response to failure in which individuals feel badly, blame themselves, and do not persist at the task because they believe they cannot succeed

Key Term Matching II: Applications, Examples, and More

Instructions: Match each key term with an application or example of the term.

Set A

KEY TERM

1. _____ psychic energy   10. _____ Oedipus complex

2. _____ Electra complex   11. _____ self-socialization

3. _____ id   12. _____ superego

4. _____ vicarious reinforcement   13. _____ reciprocal determinism

5. _____ imprinting   14. _____ systematic desensitization

6. _____ perceived self-efficacy   15. _____ ego

7. _____ erogenous zones   16. _____ child maltreatment

8. _____ behavior modification   17. _____ internalization

9. _____ ADHD

APPLICATION OR EXAMPLE

a. according to social cognitive theories, this involves children's adoption of particular goals to guide their own behavior based on their knowledge and beliefs about themselves and others

b. according to Freud, psychic energy becomes focused in these during various stages of development

c. this type of therapy is particularly useful for changing undesirable behaviors

d. this personality structure is ruled by the reality principle

e. the personality structure that is generally thought of as the conscience

f. parents' poor impulse control and their feeling of being in a power struggle in which they are the victims contribute to this

g. this type of therapy is particularly useful in the treatment of fears and phobias

h. Freud believed that this conflict was not as strong for girls as boys' conflict was for them, and thus that girls do not develop as strong a superego as do boys

i.   Bandura's "Bobo doll" study demonstrated the effectiveness of this for increasing and decreasing the likelihood that children will imitate a behavior

j.   Bandura's concept of this demonstrates his view that children play an active role in their own development

k.   according to Freud, this is initially focused on bodily needs but some of it becomes diverted and transformed into psychological needs and desires in later stages of development

l.   this ensures that the baby will stay near a source of protection and food

m.   Freud believed that, to cope with this, boys increase their identification with their fathers and thus develop a strong superego

n.   children with this syndrome have do not have as great a difficulty when there are no distractions

o.   this personality structure is most apparent in selfish behavior in which immediate gratification is sought with little or no regard for consequences

p.   Bandura proposes that an individual's _____ in various domains often operate together.

q.   this process allows for the formation of the superego

Set B

KEY TERM

18.	_____	latency period	27.	_____ exosystem
19.	_____	anal stage	28.	_____ macrosystem
20.	_____	mesosystem	29.	_____ chronosystem
21.	_____	oral stage	30.	_____ role taking
22.	_____	genital stage	31.	_____ parental-investment theory
23.	_____	ethology	32.	_____ hostile attributional bias
24.	_____	entity theory	33.	_____ mastery orientation
25.	_____	microsystem	34.	_____ incremental theory
26.	_____	phallic stage	35.	_____ helpless orientation

APPLICATION OR EXAMPLE

r.   during much of this stage of Freud's theory, the only personality structure ruling the individual is the id

s.   Carol Dweck and her colleagues have suggested that this reflects individuals' beliefs that intelligence is a fixed trait and that it cannot be changed

t.   this level of the developmental context includes the subcultural groups to which a child belongs as well as the laws and values of society

u.   during this stage of Freud's theory, sexual desires are safely hidden away in the unconscious

v.   this attempts to explain the relatively increased violence of stepparents toward stepchildren in terms of the fact that stepchildren cannot perpetuate one's genes are thus are less worthy of time, energy, and resources

w.   Selman believed this was crucial to the understanding of others' motives, thoughts, and feelings

x.   this can become a self-fulfilling prophecy, as children who possess it respond aggressively to peers, eliciting counterattacks and rejection by peers, further supporting the child's belief in others' antagonism

y.   when evaluating their own performance, children with this belief tend to focus on effort or learning rather than outcome

z.   this level of the developmental context includes parents' interactions with a child's peers

aa.   this level of the developmental context includes the age of the child when exposed to particular events

bb.   according to Freud, this stage spans the ages of 3 to 6

cc.   this level of the developmental context includes the school board and parents' workplaces

dd.   this involves attempting to understand behavior in terms of its adaptive value; for example applying the concept of imprinting to the process of human infant attachment

ee.   this stage of Freud's theory begins in adolescence

ff.   when evaluating their own performance, children with this belief tend to focus on outcome rather than effort or learning

gg.   during this stage of Freud's theory, conflict arises when parents begin to make demands on the child regarding toilet training

hh.   children who demonstrate this tend to believe that their failure is a result of insufficient effort or lack of preparation and thus that trying harder will result in success

ii.   this level of the developmental context includes a child's family and school

True/False Questions

Instructions: Indicate whether each item is true or false.

_____ 1.   Freud theorized that the source of psychic energy is the ego.

_____ 2.   According to Freud, penis envy appears during the same stage as children begin to identify with the same-sex parent.

_____ 3.   Erikson believed that individuals could get fixated in a particular stage if the need of that stage were not met.

_____ 4.   According to Erikson, unsuccessful experiences in the cognitive and social domains during childhood can lead to feelings of shame and doubt.

_____ 5.   Erikson's psychosocial stages of development have received some support from recent research on autobiographical memory.

_____ 6.   In systematic desensitization, individuals are repeatedly exposed to a fear-inducing stimulus just enough to cause them moderate, but not severe, fear.

_____ 7.   Skinner believed that everything individuals do in life is a response influenced by the outcomes of past behavior.

_____ 8.   Bandura's research with the Bobo doll is typical of research examining reciprocal determinism.

_____ 9.   Selman agreed with Piaget's belief that children under the age of six are unaware of the existence of any perspective other than their own.

_____ 10. Children with a hostile attributional bias only make hostile attributions when the intent of the perpetrator is clear.

_____ 11. Children with an entity theory of intelligence are more likely to respond to failure with a mastery orientation than with a helpless orientation.

_____ 12. Ethology focuses on behaviors that are common to all humans living in a particular culture during a particular historical era.

_____ 13. Play is considered non-adaptive by evolutionary psychologists because it delays the onset of adult behaviors, including reproduction.

_____ 14. The microsystem becomes more complex as the child grows older.

_____ 15. Societal values are included in Bronfenbrenner's mesosystem.

_____ 16. In 2003 in the Unites States, approximately 3 children in 1,000 were maltreated.

_____ 17. Individuals who experience abuse early in life are at a higher risk of heart disease than are other individuals.

_____ 18. Video games have been shown to have some cognitive benefits.

_____   19.   The heightened psychological arousal associated with exposure to media violence makes youth more likely to respond violently to provocations immediately after viewing a violent film.

_____   20.   The notion of the "poor little rich kid" appears to have no basis in fact.

Multiple-Choice Questions

1. Freud's theory is generally referred to as a theory of:
   A. psychosocial development.
   B. psychosexual development.
   C. social learning.
   D. social problem solving.

2. According to Freud, psychic energy is primarily focused on:
   A. erogenous zones.
   B. the ego.
   C. development of identity.
   D. the conscience.

3. The ego is ruled by:
   A. the conscience.
   B. the pleasure principle.
   C. conscious impulses.
   D. the reality principle.

4. According to Erikson, children who doubt their abilities or feel a general sense of shame have not resolved which of the following conflicts successfully?
   A. Autonomy vs. Shame and Doubt
   B. Initiative vs. Guilt
   C. Industry vs. Inferiority
   D. Identity vs. Role Confusion

5. Traditional learning theorists considered children to be _____ in their own development. Recent social learning theorists place an emphasis on children as _____ in their own development.
   A. active; active
   B. active; passive
   C. passive; active
   D. passive; passive

6. Which of the following is a true statement about Watson's experiment with Little Albert?
   A. It offers little in terms of practical applications.
   B. It only worked because Little Albert had a natural fear of rats.
   C. It is a good example of the effectiveness of punishment.
   D. It is considered unethical by present standards.

7. Each time two-year-old Janice hits her brother, her parents give her a "time out" with the expectation that this will cause Janice to stop hitting. This strategy is based on the principles of:
A. operant conditioning.
B. classical conditioning.
C. social learning.
D. systematic desensitization.

8. Albert Bandura's social learning theory differed from other learning theories in that it proposed that:
A. development is discontinuous.
B. reinforcement has no part in development.
C. children play an active role in their own development.
D. punishment is more important than positive reinforcement.

9. Aggressive children's hostile attributional bias occurs during which step(s) of Dodge's information-processing?
A. enacting a behavior
B. formulating a goal
C. encoding an event and interpreting social cues
D. generating strategies and evaluating likely success of strategies

10. Children who blame themselves for failure, feel badly when they fail, and do not persist when they are failing at a task are referred to as displaying:
A. poor academic competence.
B. a mastery orientation.
C. an insecure attachment.
D. a helpless pattern of motivation.

11. In a study that examined the amount of time newborn boys and girls looked at social stimuli and nonsocial stimuli, results demonstrated that:
A. *both* boys and girls primarily looked at *social* stimuli.
B. *both* boys and girls primarily looked at *nonsocial* stimuli.
C. *boys* looked longer at social stimuli than at nonsocial stimuli, whereas *girls* displayed the opposite pattern.
D. *girls* looked longer at social stimuli than at nonsocial stimuli, whereas *boys* displayed the opposite pattern.

12. The prolonged period of human children's immaturity is most interesting to which theorists?
    A. bioecological
    B. information-processing
    C. evolutionary
    D. behaviorist

13. Which of the following theories tries to account for the enormous amount of time, energy, and resources parents expend in raising their children?
    A. risk-reward
    B. parental investment
    C. Darwinian
    D. attachment

14. Which of the following lists the levels of environmental influences from closest to the child to farthest from the child?
    A. microsystem, exosystem, macrosystem
    B. macrosystem, microsystem, exosystem
    C. exosystem, microsystem, macrosystem
    D. microsystem, macrosystem, exosystem

15. The microsystem involves the:
    A. settings in which the child is not a direct participant.
    B. general beliefs, values, customs, and laws of the larger society.
    C. activities, roles, and relationships in which the child directly participates.
    D. connections among the contexts in which the child directly participates.

16. Which of the following is a true statement about the association between child maltreatment and family income?
    A. Maltreatment occurs *only* in poor families.
    B. Maltreatment rates are *associated* with *lower* family income.
    C. Maltreatment rates are *unassociated* with family income.
    D. Maltreatment rates are *associated* with *higher* family income.

17. The promising child maltreatment intervention program described in the text focused on which of the following contextual levels?
    A. exosystem
    B. macrosystem
    C. chronosystem
    D. microsystem

18. Research on the effect of media violence on children's use of aggression and violence has:
   A. clearly demonstrated that there is *no* relation between media violence and children's aggression and violence.
   B. clearly demonstrated that media violence *increases* children's aggression and violence.
   C. clearly demonstrated that media violence *decreases* children's aggression and violence.
   D. been inconclusive.

19. Carl watches a lot of TV and plays a lot of video games. About which of the following problems should Carl's parents probably be LEAST concerned?
   A. social isolation
   B. exposure to pornography
   C. exposure to violence
   D. physical inactivity

20. Which of the following is an example of an aspect of SES that occurs at the level of the chronosystem?
   A. parents' employment status
   B. changes in types of jobs over time
   C. government policies
   D. family's housing
   E. neighborhood

Essay Questions

Instructions: Answer the following essay questions on a separate sheet of paper.

1. Think about a difficult decision you have recently made or a conflict you have recently experienced – with a sibling, parent, roommate, friend, significant other, or professor. Describe the situation and the role each of your three personality structures played in this situation. In other words, according to Freud, what were the goals of your id, your ego, and your superego, and how did these goals influence the final decision or conflict resolution?

2. Describe Bandura's view of observational learning. Be sure your description includes answers to the following two questions: (1) Do children need reinforcement to be able to learn from imitation? (2) What cognitive processes are involved in such learning?

3. From the perspective of the bioecological model, describe the contexts in which you are currently developing. How are the relationships among the microsystems bi-directional? Also, how do you actively influence these contexts?

4. Give a detailed description of at least three ways in which exposure to media violence has an impact on children's aggressive and violent behavior. Additionally, provide an example of each way.

5. Which of the theories described in this chapter rang true to you? In other words, which theory made the most sense to you in terms of your own experience and your own intuition? Additionally which theory made the least sense to you? Explain your answers, and provide examples to support your point.

Answer Key

Key Term Matching I

1. i	6. o	11. b	16. d	21. hh	26. cc	31. aa
2. k	7. f	12. c	17. e	22. dd	27. ee	32. y
3. g	8. m	13. h	18. x	23. s	28. r	33. t
4. n	9. j	14. q	19. w	24. bb	29. ii	34. u
5. l	10. a	15. p	20. gg	25. ff	30. v	35. z

Key Term Matching II

1. k	6. p	11. a	16. f	21. r	26. bb	31. v
2. h	7. b	12. e	17. q	22. ee	27. cc	32. x
3. o	8. c	13. j	18. u	23. dd	28. t	33. hh
4. i	9. n	14. g	19. gg	24. ff	29. aa	34. y
5. l	10. m	15. d	20. z	25. ii	30. w	35. s

True/False Questions

1. F	6. F	11. F	16. F
2. T	7. T	12. F	17. T
3. F	8. F	13. F	18. T
4. F	9. T	14. T	19. T
5. T	10. F	15. F	20. F

Multiple-Choice Questions

1. B	6. D	11. D	16. B
2. A	7. A	12. C	17. D
3. D	8. C	13. B	18. B
4. A	9. C	14. A	19. A
5. C	10. D	15. C	20. B

CHAPTER 10
Emotional Development

Learning Objectives

Following the completion of the study of Chapter 10, you should be able to:

1. Identify the abilities that constitute emotional intelligence.

2. Explain the distinction between the views of emotion conveyed in **discrete emotions theory** and the **functionalist approach**.

3. Summarize the course of development of positive emotions and negative emotions and describe the major milestones that are involved.

4. Give examples of **self-conscious emotions** and explain the cognitive changes and social experiences that are associated with the emergence of these emotions during the second year of life.

5. Identify several factors that contribute to depression among adolescents.

6. Explain three general age-related patterns of change in the development of emotional self-regulation.

7. Name several dimensions of temperament.

8. Explain the role of temperament in children's social skills and adjustment, incorporating the concept of **goodness of fit**.

9. Discuss some of the socialization practices that parents should follow to foster their children's emotional responding.

10. Give an example of the way in which the norms, values, and circumstances of a culture or subcultural group may contribute to differences among groups in their expression of emotion.

11. Summarize major developments (including the use of **social referencing**) in children's ability to identify the emotions of others.

12. Identify milestones in children's developing ability to understand the causes of emotions.

13. List several factors associated with age-related increases in children's understanding of real and false emotions and of display rules.

14. Discuss one key piece of evidence presented in Chapter 10 that supports the view that nature and nurture interact in emotional development.

You Should Know:

Introduction

- how Mischel predicted long-term outcomes from childhood behavior.
- what emotional intelligence is, how it differs from IQ, and why it is important.

The Development of Emotions in Childhood *(summary on pg. 387 of text)*

Introduction
- how "emotions" differ from "feelings."
- the four components of emotions.

Theories on the Nature and Emergence of Emotion
- how researchers and theorists differ on the innate versus learned nature of emotions, the association between emotions and facial expressions, and the developmental progression of emotional experience.

The Emergence of Emotion in the Early Years and Childhood
- the general developmental progression of the experience and expression of positive emotions and negative emotions.
- how infants' emotions are assessed in the laboratory, and what research has indicated about the differentiation of negative emotions in infancy.
- how separation anxiety differs across environments.
- how self-conscious emotions differ from other emotions, in terms of their characteristics and their development.
- how caregivers can encourage children to experience guilt over shame.
- how the causes and experience of emotions differ across childhood and adolescence.
- the extent to which depression is experienced by children and adolescents and what various theories suggest about its causes.

Box 10.1: Individual Differences: Gender Differences in Adolescent Depression
- how rates with which adolescents experience depression differ across boys and girls and the possible causes of these differences.

Regulation of Emotion (*summary on pg. 390 of text*)

The Development of Emotional Regulation

- what emotional regulation entails, and how infants and young children begin to regulate their own emotions.
- how older children regulate their emotions differently than do younger children, and why older children's selection of strategies differs from that of younger children.

The Relation of Emotional Regulation to Social Competence and Adjustment

- how and why emotional regulation is associated with social competence and adjustment.

Individual Differences in Emotion and Its Regulation (*summary on pg. 398 of text*)

Temperament

- what temperament is and how Thomas and Chess, as well as more recent researchers, have characterized infants and children.
- how early temperament is associated with later temperament and later adjustment.
- what the concept of goodness of fit is and how it relates to adjustment.

Box 10.2: A Closer Look: Measurement of Temperament

- the multiple ways in which temperament has been assessed and the advantages and disadvantages of the various methods.
- what behavioral inhibition is, how it has been assessed, and how it is associated with later behavioral patterns.

Children's Emotional Development in the Family (*summary on pg. 401 of text*)

Introduction

- how temperament and personality are related.

Quality of the Child's Relationships with Parents

- the ways in which the quality of the parent-child relationship is associated with emotional development.

Parental Socialization of Children's Emotional Responding

- the ways in which parents have a direct and indirect influence on their children's emotional response.
- how parents' expression of emotion, parents' reactions to children's emotions, and parental conversations about emotions are associated with children's emotional responding and later adjustment.

- how children's own behavior may affect parents' expression of emotion, parents' reactions to children's emotions, and parental discussion of emotions.

Culture and Children's Emotional Development *(summary on pg. 403 of text)*

- how the expression of emotion varies across cultures and subcultures and how this is associated with cultural differences in parenting practices and cultural values.
- how the association between emotional responses and adjustment is similar and different across cultures.

Children's Understanding of Emotion *(summary on pg. 409 of text)*

Identifying the Emotions of Others
- the developmental progression of children's ability to discriminate and identify others' emotions and why these are important skills.
- how the ability to discriminate identify emotions has been studied.

Understanding the Causes of Emotion
- the developmental progression of children's understanding of the causes of emotions and why this is an important skill.

Children's Understanding of Real and False Emotions
- the developmental progression of children's understanding of the difference between real and false emotions.
- how social factors influence children's understanding of real and false emotions.

Understanding Simultaneous and Ambivalent Emotions
- the developmental progression of children's understanding of simultaneous and ambivalent emotions.

Key Term Matching I: Definitions

Instructions: Match each key term with its definition.

KEY TERM

1.	_____	personality	9. _____	behavioral inhibition
2.	_____	self-conscious emotions	10. _____	separation anxiety
3.	_____	goodness of fit	11. _____	social competence
4.	_____	discrete emotions theory	12. _____	display rules
5.	_____	social referencing	13. _____	emotional intelligence
6.	_____	temperament	14. _____	emotional self-regulation
7.	_____	emotion	15. _____	social smiles
8.	_____	socialization	16. _____	functionalist approach

DEFINITION

a.   the pattern of emotional and behavioral tendencies, beliefs and interests, and intellectual capabilities that characterize an individual

b.   a social group's informal norms about when, where, and how much one should show emotions

c.   the view that emotions are distinct from one another and are evident from early in life

d.   differences in aspects of emotional, motor, and attention reactivity and self-regulation that are apparent from early in life

e.   the degree to which an individual's temperament is suited to their particular environment

f.   feeling of distress that infants experience when separated from an attachment figure

g.   emotions that relate to an individual's sense of self and an awareness of others' reactions

h.   the process of controlling one's emotions, including the associated subjective feelings, physiological processes, behaviors, and cognitions

i.   the ability to achieve one's goals in social situations while maintaining positive relations with others

j.   the view that the purpose of emotions is to promote action toward a goal

k.   a dimension of temperament that involves fearful distress, particularly in novel situations

l.   smiles that are directed at people

m.   a set of abilities that are key to competent social functioning

n.   the indirect and direct influences of parents, teachers, and other aspects of the environment on children's standards, values, and ways of thinking and feeling

o.   infants' use of a caregiver's facial or vocal cues to interpret a novel or ambiguous situation

p.   characterized by a motivational force, subjective experience, changes in physiology, and cognitions

Key Term Matching II: Applications, Examples, and More

Instructions: Match each key term with an application or example of the term.

KEY TERM

1. _____ separation anxiety	9. _____ goodness of fit
2. _____ emotional intelligence	10. _____ emotion
3. _____ social smiles	11. _____ social competence
4. _____ personality	12. _____ behavioral inhibition
5. _____ discrete emotions theory	13. _____ functionalist approach
6. _____ display rules	14. _____ social referencing
7. _____ socialization	15. _____ emotional self-regulation
8. _____ self-conscious emotions	16. _____ temperament

APPLICATION OR EXAMPLE

a. these emerge as early as 6 or 7 weeks of age and do not refer to happiness experienced as a result of being able to control an object

b. children who have a high activity level, have intense reactions to negative stimuli, and are not easily distractible and children who are generally cheerful and easy to calm differ in this

c. when infants begin to do this at about 8 to 12 months of age, it is an indication that they can relate others' emotional expressions to events in the environment

d. researchers holding this view would point to the association between anger and an individual's movement to eliminate obstacles

e. this predicts how well individuals do in life even to a greater extent than does IQ

f. a child who crawls away from his caregiver is probably less likely to experience this than a child whose caregiver leaves the room

g. happiness, anger, and sadness are *not* examples of these

h. young children who must rely on caregivers to settle them down have not fully developed this

i. this has its roots in temperament, but is also shaped by the environment

j. theorists disagree about the extent to which this involves cognition as well as whether the experience of this is entirely innate or partially learned

k. infants who are high in this tend to be less social and less positive at age four

l. even a child with a difficult temperament can thrive if the environment is satisfactory in terms of this

m. children with this are good at regulating their emotions, tend to use cognitive methods of controlling their emotions, and tend to be able to delay gratification

n. parents' expression of emotion with their children and parents' reactions to their children's emotional expression are two examples of how parents accomplish this

o. researchers holding this view would *disagree* with the statement, "Infants only experience excitement and distress, and they must learn how to express these emotions"

p. examples of these include those with a prosocial motive, when one doesn't want to hurt another's feelings, and those with a self-protective motive, when one doesn't want to look bad in front of others

True/False Questions

Instructions: Indicate whether each item is true or false.

_____ 1. Rational thinking is an important part of emotional intelligence.

_____ 2. Researchers generally agree on which emotions are innate and which ones require experience.

_____ 3. Parents are quite accurate at identifying specific emotions in their young infants.

_____ 4. Infants tend to experience less separation anxiety when they are the ones who do the departing, as when they walk away from their parent, than when their parents do the departing.

_____ 5. Anger and other self-conscious emotions emerge in the second year of life.

_____ 6. Situations likely to induce pride in Western cultures may induce embarrassment or shame in non-Western cultures.

_____ 7. As they develop, children's growing understanding of people and events affects the types of things that make them laugh.

_____ 8. Research has clearly demonstrated that depression is entirely caused by individuals' personal vulnerability rather than simply by stressful external factors.

_____ 9. Depression in adolescent boys often co-occurs with behavioral problems, and thus adults may fail to see their depressive symptoms.

_____ 10. Parents' expectations of children to manage their own emotions contribute to the development of children's emotional regulation.

_____ 11. It is likely that most differences in emotional reactivity are due to differences in socialization.

_____ 12. Initial studies by Thomas and Chess classified 40% of infants as difficult.

_____ 13. Activation of the right frontal lobe has been shown to be associated with approach behavior and positive affect, whereas activation of the left frontal lobe has been shown to be associated with anxiety in novel situations and inhibition.

_____ 14. Children's temperaments may affect parenting practices, which may in turn affect children's style.

_____ 15. Twin and adoption studies demonstrate that all aspects of temperament are genetically based.

_____ 16. Parental socialization of emotion involves parents' own expression of emotion, parents' reactions to their children's emotions, and parents' conversations with their children regarding emotion.

_____   17.   Children's emotional responses are largely temperamental, and thus there is little parents can do to explicitly teach children how to respond emotionally.

_____   18.   Cultural differences in values probably cause the same parenting behaviors to have different consequences for children's social and emotional well-being in different cultures.

_____   19.   Children's ability to label others' emotions is essentially unrelated to their social competence.

_____   20.   Children are able to identify others' negative emotions before others' positive emotions and are able to understand the causes of other's negative emotions before they can understand the causes of others' positive emotions

Multiple-Choice Questions

1. Emotional intelligence includes:
   A. the ability to regulate one's emotions.
   B. the ability to delay gratification.
   C. knowledge about what makes people experience various emotions.
   D. the ability to identify one's own emotional state.
   E. A and D
   F. all of the above

2. Young infants tend to smile at all of the following EXCEPT:
   A. at people.
   B. at interesting objects.
   C. when they can control an event.
   D. Young infants tend to smile at all of the above.

3. Which of the following children is *least* likely to experience separation anxiety?
   A. 11-month-old Tara, who crawls away from her mother to explore a novel toy.
   B. 10-month-old Lee, whose mother leaves him in his crib.
   C. 13-month-old Bethany, who is blind and hears her mother leave the room.
   D. 6-month-old Simon, whose mother leaves the room in which he is playing.
   E. All of these children are equally likely to experience separation anxiety.
   F. Tara (A) and Simon (D) are both unlikely to experience separation anxiety.
   G. Bethany (C) and Simon (D) are both unlikely to experience separation anxiety.

4. Which of the following is NOT a self-conscious emotion?
   A. pride
   B. shame
   C. embarrassment
   D. fear

5. Juan is jumping on the bed and mistakenly falls and kicks his sister. He feels terrible and regrets jumping on the bed. He is trying desperately to make her feel better by hugging and kissing her. Juan is primarily experiencing which of the following emotions?
   A. anger
   B. embarrassment
   C. guilt
   D. shame

6. Which of the following is a true statement about rates of depression and negative emotion in childhood and adolescence?
   A. Typical adolescents experience only a mild increase in negative emotions.
   B. Rates of clinical depression are very high during childhood.
   C. Changes in emotionality during adolescence are entirely due to hormonal changes.
   D. Rates of depression do not change from childhood to adolescence.
   E. none of the above

7. As children get older, they increasingly regulate their negative emotions by:
   A. relying on their parents.
   B. using cognitive strategies.
   C. having temper tantrums.
   D. using more physical self-soothing techniques.

8. Thomas and Chess labeled babies who were generally cheerful, who adjusted to new situations without much trouble, and who were regular in their routines as:
   A. slow-to-warm-up.
   B. difficult.
   C. easy.
   D. quick-to-calm-down.

9. Infants' anger and frustration, especially when being prevented from doing what they want is referred to as:
   A. surgency.
   B. irritable distress.
   C. rhythmicity.
   D. fearful distress.
   E. low positive affect.

10. Children high in fearful distress, particularly in novel or stressful situations, are considered to be:
    A. behaviorally inhibited.
    B. irritable.
    C. high in anger/frustration.
    D. easy.

11. Children with behavioral inhibition are more likely than children with other temperaments to exhibit which of the following as adolescents or young adults?
   A. popularity
   B. getting in trouble with the law
   C. impulsivity
   D. anxiety

12. Goodness of fit describes which of the following associations?
   A. the effect of children's temperament on later social functioning
   B. the interaction between children's temperament and their social (e.g., family) environment
   C. the effect of family environment on children's temperament
   D. the interaction between children's temperamental regulation and their temperamental emotionality

13. Which of the following is a true statement about the risk of clinical depression?
   A. Adolescents from wealthy families are at higher risk than those from poor families.
   B. Euro-American adolescents are at higher risk than Hispanic-American adolescents.
   C. Male adolescents are at higher risk than female adolescents.
   D. All of the above statements are true.
   E. None of the above statements is true.

14. A nine-month-old infant is habituated to pictures of people expressing happiness. The infant is then presented with a picture of a person expressing anger. The infant is likely to:
   A. display no renewed interest in the pictures, as infants this young are unable to differentiate between emotions.
   B. dishabituate to the new picture, but not comprehend the difference in meaning between the first set of pictures and the new picture.
   C. dishabituate to the new picture and comprehend the emotional meaning of the facial expressions.
   D. cry, as the removal of the happy face is likely to elicit fear in the infant.

15. Children's use of a parent's facial, vocal, or gestural cues to decide on how to deal with ambiguous situations is referred to as:
   A. social referencing.
   B. emotional regulation.
   C. self-socialization.
   D. display rules.

16. Does social referencing involve infants' emotional *and* behavioral responses to ambiguous events?
   A. Yes, it involves *both* emotional and behavioral responses.
   B. No, it involves emotional responses, but not behavioral responses.
   C. No, it involves behavioral responses, but not emotional responses.
   D. No, it involves *neither* emotional nor behavioral responses.

17. Three-year-old Ian is told a story about Jimmy, a boy who loves to go to the park. Jimmy is in the car with his father, and they are on their way to the park. When Ian is asked how Jimmy is feeling, Ian is likely to expect which of the following emotions?
   A. sadness
   B. shame
   C. happiness
   D. Ian will be unable to predict Jimmy's emotion.

18. Which of the following is an ability of the typical fifth grader?
   A. identifying the causes of others' negative emotions
   B. labeling self-conscious emotions in other people
   C. identifying the causes of others' positive emotions
   D. a good understanding of how memories of past emotional events can trigger the same emotions
   E. all of the above
   F. none of the above

19. Which of the following is NOT an example of the use of a display rule?
   A. Sam pretends to be happy when he takes a bite of his friend's cooking concoction.
   B. Nilda appears sad when her friend is leaving even though she is relieved to have her go.
   C. Ross is excited about making a mess in his playroom but gets upset when his mother comes in the room and gets angry.
   D. Emma smiles in front of her classmates even though she has just lost the spelling bee.

20. Which of the following children's emotions would be the *most difficult* for other children to understand?
   A. Mia, who feels disappointment at getting a sweater for her birthday, but who puts on a happy face anyway.
   B. J.T, who feels sad at a happy occasion (e.g., birthday party).
   C. Kerry, who is saddened by a reminder of her pets' death.
   D. Jing, who is happy because he is going to the park with his friend.

Essay Questions

Instructions: Answer the following essay questions on a separate sheet of paper.

1. Describe the impact of the sociocultural context on the development and experience of emotions, including basic emotions and self-conscious emotions. Provide supportive examples.

2. Describe an event that would evoke fear in children of each of the following ages: infancy, toddlerhood, preschool age, and late childhood. Describe how children of each of these ages would be likely to attempt to regulate their fear.

3. Think about an infant you know or use the information your parents have told you about what you were like as an infant. Would the parents of this infant describe the infant (or you) as an easy, difficult, or slow-to-warm-up child? What characteristics does this infant exhibit that cause you to classify him or her in that way?

4. Describe the three ways that parents socialize their children's emotional development. Give an example of each. In addition, for each of the three paths, give an example of how children may influence their parents.

5. Why is it so important for social competence that children can identify their own emotions? In addition, why is it so important for social competence that children can identify other people's emotions? Provide supportive examples.

Answer Key

Key Term Matching I

1. a	4. c	7. p	10. f	13. m	16. j
2. g	5. o	8. n	11. i	14. h	
3. e	6. d	9. k	12. b	15. l	

Key Term Matching II

1. f	4. i	7. n	10. j	13. d	16. b
2. e	5. o	8. g	11. m	14. c	
3. a	6. p	9. l	12. k	15. h	

True/False Questions

1. F	6. T	11. F	16. T
2. F	7. T	12. F	17. F
3. F	8. F	13. F	18. T
4. T	9. T	14. T	19. F
5. F	10. T	15. F	20. T

Multiple-Choice Questions

1. F	6. A	11. D	16. A
2. D	7. B	12. B	17. C
3. F	8. C	13. E	18. E
4. D	9. B	14. C	19. C
5. C	10. A	15. A	20. A

CHAPTER 11

Attachment to Others and Development of Self

Learning Objectives

Following the completion of the study of Chapter 11, you should be able to:

1. Summarize the central ideas of attachment theory, as developed by John Bowlby, including the concept of the **secure base**.

2. Identify the four phases in the initial development of attachment.

3. Explain what an **internal working model** of attachment means and how it relates to adult attachment models.

4. Describe the Strange Situation behaviors of infants in each of the four attachment categories: secure attachment, insecure/resistant (or ambivalent) attachment, insecure/avoidant attachment, and disorganized/disoriented attachment.

5. Discuss the role of parental sensitivity in the development of secure attachment.

6. Describe the long-term effects of security of attachment.

7. Outline the development of the concept of the self in infancy, childhood, and adolescence, including the major developmental milestones.

8. Explain the four possible outcomes that result from the resolution of the crisis of identity versus identity confusion, as postulated by Erik Erikson.

9. Identify the five components of children's ethnic identity.

10. Summarize the development of ethnic identity from childhood through adolescence.

11. List the developmental milestones in the process of self-labeling and disclosure among **sexual-minority youth**.

12. Discuss the special challenges faced by sexual-minority youth in identity formation.

13. Identity several factors that affect children's **self-esteem**.

14. Compare levels of self-esteem among majority and minority children.

15. Discuss the complexities inherent in cross-cultural comparisons of self-esteem.

You Should Know:

Introduction

- the types of observations child-care professionals were making in the 1930s and 1940s of children growing up in institutions and foster care.

- how these observations and early research changed the predominant view of the important dimensions of caregiving and sparked the important writings of John Bowlby.

The Caregiver-Child Attachment Relationship (*summary on pg. 426 of text*)

Introduction

- what early research was conducted on issues of attachment and early social interaction and how the findings informed future research.

Attachment Theory

- Bowlby's conception of attachment and how the caregiver is regarded in his attachment theory.

- the phases through which attachment is proposed to develop and what the usual outcome of these phases is.

Measurement of Attachment Security

- the general features of the most commonly-used laboratory test for assessing infants' attachment to their primary caregiver and why Ainsworth believed these features were important in the assessment of attachment behavior.

- the infant behaviors that are observed during the Strange Situation, the attachment categories into which infants are categorized, and how infants' behaviors are used to place infants into categories.

Box 11.1: Individual Differences: Parental Attachment Status

- what adult attachment models are and how they are assessed.

- how parents' attachment classification is associated with their children's attachment style and why these associations exist.

Cultural Variations in Attachment

- how attachment patterns are similar across cultures, as well as how they differ.

- why the behavior of infants in the Strange Situation may differ across cultures and what the possible explanations for these differences are.

Factors Associated with the Security of Children's Attachment

- why parental sensitivity is believed to be crucial to the development of a secure attachment and how mothers of securely attached infants and mothers of insecurely-attached infants differ.

- what role infants' own temperament plays in their attachment style.

Box 11.2: Applications: Interventions and Attachment

- why interventions enable researchers to examine the causal nature of parental sensitivity on infant attachment, as well as what intervention research has demonstrated about this issue.

Does Security of Attachment Have Long-Term Effects?

- how attachment style in infancy is associated with later psychological, social, and cognitive functioning.

- what controversy exists about the nature of this association, what research has been done to examine this issue, and what this research has demonstrated.

Conceptions of the Self (*summary on pg. 435 of text*)

Introduction

- what the self is and why the development of conceptions of the self is important to psychological functioning.

The Development of Conceptions of Self

- how a sense of self emerges throughout the first three years of life and what empirical evidence has informed psychologists' understanding of this development.

- how children and adolescents of different ages typically describe themselves and what these descriptions reflect about their conceptions of self.

- what developmental changes influence the development of children's and adolescents' conceptions of self.

- how adolescents' egocentrism influences their beliefs about themselves.

Identity in Adolescence

- Erikson's conception of identity formation, the types of negative outcomes that are possible in this process, and why Erikson believed in the importance of a psychosocial moratorium.

- how research on identity formation has followed from Erikson's theory and what identity statuses have been identified.

- how individuals' identity status is associated with their functioning.

- how identity formation is influenced by parenting behavior, adolescents' own behavior, and the larger culture.

Ethnic Identity (*summary on pg. 439 of text*)

Introduction
- what ethnic identity is and why it is important to consider it when discussing identity development.

Ethnic Identity in Childhood
- the components of ethnic identity and how ethnic identity develops during childhood.

Ethnic Identity in Adolescence
- the difficulties associated with identity development for ethnic-minority youth.
- the three phases involved in the common pattern of ethnic-identity development, as well as the alternatives to this pattern.
- the association between ethnic identity and adjustment for minority and majority youth.

Sexual Identity or Orientation (*summary on pg. 443 of text*)

The Origins of Youths' Sexual Identity
- how heredity and environment influence the development of sexual identity.

Sexual Identity in Sexual-Minority Youth
- the challenges many sexual-minority youth face in the development of a sexual identity.
- the developmental milestones of the coming-out process.
- what the consequences of coming out may be in terms of family and peer relationships and other measures of adjustment.

Self-Esteem (*summary on pg. 449 of text*)

Introduction
- what self-esteem is and why its study is important.

Sources of Self-Esteem
- how self-esteem is generally assessed.
- how heredity contributes to individual differences in self-esteem.

- how parents and peers influence children's self-esteem and how their degree of influence varies depending on the age of the child.

- how children's appearance and competence, as well as children's school organization and neighborhood, are associated with self-esteem.

Self-Esteem in Minority Children

- the patterns of self-esteem for ethnic-minority children and how they compare to those of ethnic-majority children.

- how ethnic identity influences the self-esteem of ethnic-minority children.

Culture and Self-Esteem

- how the form and function of self-esteem, as well as its sources, differ across cultures.

- how cultural differences can influence individuals' reports of self-esteem.

Key Term Matching I: Definitions

Instructions: Match each key term with its definition.

Set A

KEY TERM

1. _____ imaginary audience
2. _____ self
3. _____ moratorium status
4. _____ identity-achievement status
5. _____ adult attachment models
6. _____ Strange Situation
7. _____ identity-diffusion status
8. _____ secure base

9. _____ foreclosure status
10. _____ personal fable
11. _____ attachment theory
12. _____ insecure attachment
13. _____ social comparison
14. _____ identity versus identity confusion
15. _____ secure attachment

DEFINITION

a. Erikson's psychosocial stage of development that occurs during adolescence in which the crisis involves the construction of a coherent identity

b. a method developed by Mary Ainsworth to assess infants' attachments to their primary caregivers

c. adolescents' belief that they, and especially their feelings, are unique and special

d. a pattern of attachment in which a child has a relatively poor-quality relationship with the attachment figure

e. the notion that an attachment figure's presence provides a child with a sense of safety and confidence that enables the child to explore the environment

f. a conceptual system consisting of one's thoughts and attitudes about oneself

g. the process of judging oneself against the psychological, behavioral, or physical functioning of others in order to evaluate oneself

h. working models of attachment relationships that guide parents' attachments with their own children and are believed to be based on their perceptions of their own childhood experiences

i.   the identity-status category in which an individual does not have any firm commitments but is exploring various options

j.   a pattern of attachment in which a child has a high-quality relationship with the attachment figure

k.   the identity-status category in which an individual has explored various options and has made an autonomous commitment to personal decisions such as ideology, occupation, and sexual behavior

l.   a theory that hypothesizes that children are biologically predisposed to form attachments with their caregivers as a means of increasing their chances of survival

m.   the identity-status category in which an individual does not have any firm commitments and is not making progress toward them

n.   the identity-status category in which an individual has not engaged in any identity exploration and has established an identity based on the choices or values of others

o.   adolescents' belief that everyone else is focused on the adolescent's appearance and behavior

Set B

KEY TERM

16. _____ negative identity

17. _____ parental sensitivity

18. _____ identity confusion

19. _____ self-esteem

20. _____ insecure/avoidant attachment

21. _____ insecure/resistant attachment

22. _____ disorganized/disoriented attachment

23. _____ internal working model of attachment

24. _____ sexual orientation

25. _____ attachment

26. _____ psychosocial moratorium

27. _____ ethnic identity

28. _____ identity foreclosure

29. _____ sexual-minority youth

DEFINITION

p.　close, enduring emotional bond with a specific person

q.　one's overall evaluation of the worth of the self and the feelings associated with that evaluation

r.　a crucial factor contributing to the security of an infant's attachment that includes responsive caregiving when children are distressed

s.　an identity that represents the opposite of what is valued by people around the adolescent

t.　a time-out period in which an adolescent can explore activities that lead to self-discovery without having to take on any adult roles

u.　a pattern of attachment in which a child appears to have no consistent way of coping with the Strange Situation and thus behaves in a confused or contradictory manner

v.　a mental representation of the self, of attachment figures, and of relationships in general that is a result of experiences with caregivers

w.　an incomplete and sometimes incoherent sense of self that results from an unsuccessful resolution of Erikson's identity versus identity-confusion stage

x.　premature commitment to an identity without adequately considering other choices

y.   a pattern of attachment in which a child is clingy and stays close to the caregiver rather than exploring the environment

z.   young individuals who experience same-sex attractions

aa.   an individual's sense of belonging to an ethnic group

bb.   an individual's preference in regard to males or females as the object of erotic feelings

cc.   a pattern of attachment in which a child appears to be indifferent towards the caregiver and may stay away from the caregiver

Key Term Matching II: Applications, Examples, and More

Instructions: Match each key term with an application or example of the term.

Set A

KEY TERM

1. _____ social comparison

2. _____ Strange Situation

3. _____ identity-achievement status

4. _____ identity-diffusion status

5. _____ self

6. _____ attachment theory

7. _____ moratorium status

8. _____ secure base

9. _____ personal fable

10. _____ imaginary audience

11. _____ adult attachment models

12. _____ foreclosure status

13. _____ secure attachment

APPLICATION OR EXAMPLE

a.   a child whose caregiver does not serve this function may be unable to fully explore the environment, thereby decreasing opportunities for learning

b.   individuals with this identity status tend to believe that authority figures should make decisions for them

c.   children who exhibited this pattern of attachment as infants tend to have closer, more harmonious relationships with their peers than do other children

d.   this is generally assessed by asking adults to discuss their early childhood attachments and how they believe those early relationships have shaped them

e.   this belief causes adolescents to be preoccupied with what others think of them

f.   elementary-school children's engagement in this causes them to refine their conceptions of self to include attention to discrepancies between their own and others' behavior and characteristics

g.   an emerging understanding of this is apparent when a child succeeds at the "rouge test" and makes movements toward wiping the spot off of his or her own face rather than off of the image in the mirror

h.   this theory was proposed by John Bowlby

i. individuals with this identity status tend to be high in self-esteem and high in anxiety, and they tend to move into identity-achievement status

j. in modern, Western cultures, individuals who have attained this identity status tend to be more socially mature and more highly motivated than their peers

k. individuals with this identity status tend to be the most at-risk for drug abuse

l. during this, the infant's behaviors, including attempts to seek closeness with the caregiver, resistance to or avoidance of the caregiver, and interactions with the caregiver from a distance, are observed

m. an adolescent who says to his or her parents, "But you don't understand how it feels to be a teenager," is demonstrating this form of egocentrism

Set B

KEY TERM

14. _____ psychosocial moratorium

15. _____ sexual-minority youth

16. _____ parental sensitivity

17. _____ insecure/avoidant attachment

18. _____ attachment

19. _____ identity foreclosure

20. _____ internal working model of attachment

21. _____ identity confusion

22. _____ self-esteem

23. _____ negative identity

24. _____ insecure/resistant attachment

25. _____ ethnic identity

26. _____ disorganized/disoriented attachment

APPLICATION OR EXAMPLE

n   Erikson believed the adoption of this is some adolescents' means of getting noticed by their parents when other attempts have failed

o.   Erikson argued for the importance of this in modern society because of the complexity of achieving an identity

p.   parents who do not read their infants' signals correctly and do not respond appropriately to a baby who is crying versus smiling would be considered to be low in this

q.   the mothers of infants who display this pattern of attachment have been found to be inconsistent in their caregiving and are often anxious or overwhelmed

r.   in the Strange Situation, infants with this pattern of attachment often ignore their caregivers when they enter the room following a separation episode and ignore or turn away from them when they are in the room

s.   although it is often assumed that minority children have poorer _____ than majority children, this is generally not the case, perhaps because of minority cultures' strong and positive ethnic identity

t.   as a result of this, if children's caregivers are unresponsive and unavailable, children may hold negative perceptions of themselves and may believe that all relationships will be negative and unfulfilling

u.   this includes the degree to which individuals associate their thinking, perceptions, feelings, and behavior with membership in their ethnic group

v.   an example of this is an individual who becomes a minister simply because his parent is one

w.   adolescents in this state often feel lost, isolated, or depressed

x.   the security of this appears to have many short- and long-term consequences for children's adjustment

y.   this attachment category is often associated with a history of parental abuse

z.   for these individuals, the question of personal sexual identity is often confusing and painful

True/False Questions

Instructions: Indicate whether each item is true or false.

_____   1.   Observations of children in orphanages in the 1930s and 1940s were the basis for research on identity and self-esteem.

_____   2.   The general idea of a secure base is that a trusted caregiver always stays within an arm's reach of an infant or toddler to ensure that the child feels safe.

_____   3.   Bowlby believed that children's internal working models of attachment continue to guide individuals throughout life, influencing the types of interpersonal relationships individuals seek out and find as adults.

_____   4.   Contemporary developmentalists consider Ainsworth's Strange Situation artificial and no longer use this method to classify infants into attachment categories.

_____   5.   Infants who are clingy during the Strange Situation and cry when their mothers leave, but then refuse their mothers' offers of comfort are categorized as insecure/resistant.

_____   6.   The greater closeness and physical intimacy of Japanese mothers and infants, in comparison to U.S. mothers and infants, may explain the difference in proportions of insecure/resistant and insecure/avoidant infants in the two cultures.

_____   7.   Both experimental studies and twin studies have demonstrated the causal link between children's environments and their attachments.

_____   8.   There is clear evidence of the existence of a sensitive period for parental bonding.

_____   9.   The self includes one's thoughts about one's internal characteristics, one's social characteristics, and one's physical being.

_____   10. It is nearly impossible to assess whether preverbal children truly have a sense of themselves as beings separate from their parents.

_____   11. The typical parental practice of providing evaluative descriptions (e.g., "You're so smart") to young children contributes to their expanding self image.

_____   12. The unrealistic positivity in children's sense of self that is common during the preschool years is referred to as the personal fable.

_____   13. The emergence of abstract thinking during adolescence enables adolescents to think of themselves in terms of abstract characteristics.

_____   14. Psychosocial moratorium is often a luxury reserved for those who can attend college.

_____   15. An individual who does not have any firm commitments and is not making progress toward them is considered to be in identity foreclosure.

_____ 16.   Shortly after children are able to label themselves as belonging to an ethnic group, they understand that ethnicity is a lasting feature of the self.

_____ 17.   Biological factors are a strong influence on individuals' sexual orientation.

_____ 18.   Compared to heterosexual youth, sexual-minority youth are more at risk for suicide, problems with substance abuse, school-related problems, and depression.

_____ 19.   The most important influence on children's self-esteem is their ethnic identity.

_____ 20.   The transition from elementary school to junior high school is associated with a decline in self-esteem.

Multiple-Choice Questions

1. Bowlby proposed that newborns are in which phase of the development of attachment?
   A. attachment-in-the-making
   B. clear-cut attachment
   C. preattachment
   D. reciprocal relationships

2. Bowlby proposed that individuals' internal working models of attachment include mental representations of:
   A. attachment figures.
   B. the self.
   C. relationships in general.
   D. both A and B.
   E. both A and C.
   F. all of the above.

3. Which of the following is NOT characteristic of securely-attached infants in the Strange Situation?
   A. plays alone with the toys in the room
   B. is easily comforted by mother when upset
   C. becomes distressed when mother leaves the room
   D. fails to greet mother when she returns to the room
   E. Both C and D are uncharacteristic of securely attached infants.

4. Adults' working models of attachment are:
   A. based on adults' perceptions of their own childhood experiences.
   B. assessed by observing adults with their own parents.
   C. only held by adults who had secure attachments to their own parents.
   D. unrelated to their children's attachments to them.

5. Which of the following can have an impact on infants' behavior in the Strange Situation?
   A. parental sensitivity
   B. cultural value placed on infants' dependency on their mothers
   C. prior experience with unfamiliar people and situations
   D. both A and B
   E. all of the above

6. Mothers who are able to read their infants' signals and respond to them appropriately are likely to have infants who are:
   A. depressed.
   B. securely attached.
   C. slow-to-warm-up.
   D. disorganized/disoriented.

7. Which of the following is a true statement about the long-term association between security of attachment in infancy and later social and emotional competence?
   A. There is a clear causal long-term association.
   B. There is some evidence that the association is causal, but there is also evidence that current attachment security is the relevant factor.
   C. It is clear that the association is not a causal one.
   D. There is a clear causal association, but only over short periods of time.

8. Parental bonding refers to:
   A. the relationship between parents and children that develops over time.
   B. parents' "maternal instinct" that allows them to sense what is in their children's best interest.
   C. the extent to which parents are sensitive to their infants' needs.
   D. the deep emotional tie of parents to their children that develops shortly after birth.

9. All of the following are considered indications of a child's sense of self EXCEPT:
   A. separation distress.
   B. anger at loss of control of movement of a mobile.
   C. crying when hungry.
   D. attempting to engage adults by handing them objects.

10. Children who attempt to wipe the rouge off their own face when they are asked to clean the face of the child in the mirror:
    A. are demonstrating that they possess a sense of self.
    B. are securely attached to their primary caregiver.
    C. have a great deal of experience with make-up.
    D. have higher self-esteem than other children.

11. Which of the following is more likely to be a characteristic of a ten-year-old child's sense of self than a five-year-old child's sense of self?
    A. focused on observable characteristics
    B. involves others' evaluations of them
    C. closely tied to actual behavior
    D. based on physical attributes

12. At what age do the inconsistencies people perceive in their personalities start to bother them?
    A. early childhood
    B. late childhood
    C. early adolescence
    D. adolescence

13. Owen is an adolescent who doesn't know who he is or what he wants to make of his life. He feels isolated and depressed. Erikson would say that Owen:
    A. has a negative identity.
    B. is in a state of identity confusion.
    C. is experiencing identity foreclosure.
    D. is in a state of moratorium.
    E. has a coherent identity.

14. A period in which an adolescent can discover herself and not be expected to take on adult roles is referred to as a(n):
    A. state of identity confusion.
    B. identity achievement.
    C. moratorium.
    D. foreclosed identity.
    E. negative identity.

15. Research has indicated that adolescents in which of the following states are most at risk for drug abuse?
    A. identity diffusion
    B. moratorium
    C. foreclosure
    D. identity achievement

16. At what age do individuals start to develop meaningful ethnic labels (e.g., "I'm Mexican because my parents come from Mexico)?
  A. preschool
  B. early school years
  C. late school years
  D. early adolescence

17. Individuals' preferences in regard to males or females as the objects of erotic feelings are referred to as their:
  A. ethnic identity.
  B. gender identity.
  C. sexual orientation.
  D. gender role.

18. Which of the following is NOT true of sexual-minority youth?
  A. They tend to be confident about disclosing their sexual orientation to friends and family.
  B. They may have to contend with parental anger, disappointment, or denial.
  C. They are more likely than heterosexual youth to report losses of friendships.
  D. They are at increased risk of attempted suicide in comparison to heterosexual youth.

19. How are children's peer acceptance and self-esteem associated?
  A. Children's self-esteem influences how well-accepted they are by their peers.
  B. Children's peer acceptance influences their self-esteem.
  C. Both of the above patterns of association are accurate.
  D. Neither of the above patterns of association is accurate.

20. Which of the following is NOT a true statement about the self-esteem of ethnic minority children in comparison to Euro-American children?
  A. The self-esteem of some ethnic-minority children is negatively affected by the increased prevalence of living in poverty.
  B. The self-esteem of some ethnic-minority children is negatively affected by their strong ethnic identity.
  C. The self-esteem of some ethnic-minority children is positively affected by their parents' encouragement of closeness and connection with the family.
  D. The reported self-esteem of some ethnic minorities is relatively low due to their cultural motivation toward being self-critical.
  E. All of the above are true statements.

Essay Questions

Instructions: Answer the following essay questions on a separate sheet of paper.

1. What is strange about the Strange Situation? Why is this situation so effective in assessing the quality of infant-caregiver security?

2. What is a sense of self? Describe three indicators that a child has developed a sense of self. Provide examples of each.

3. Describe Erikson's concept of identity. What is a successful identity? Give an example of an adolescent who has achieved this state. Also, describe and give an example of an individual in each of the following identity states: (1) identity confusion, (2) identity foreclosure, (3) negative identity, and (4) moratorium.

4. How does sociocultural context influence the coming-out process and its consequences for sexual-minority youth? Give three supportive examples.

5. Describe how an individual's identity is associated with his or her self-esteem. Are these concepts the same thing? Why or why not? Provide examples as necessary to support your argument.

Answer Key

Key Term Matching I

1. o	6. b	11. l	16. s	21. y	26. t
2. f	7. m	12. d	17. r	22. u	27. aa
3. i	8. e	13. g	18. w	23. v	28. x
4. k	9. n	14. a	19. q	24. bb	29. z
5. h	10. c	15. j	20. cc	25. p	

Key Term Matching II

1. f	5. g	9. m	13. c	17. r	21. w	25. u
2. l	6. h	10. e	14. o	18. x	22. s	26. y
3. j	7. i	11. d	15. z	19. v	23. n	
4. k	8. a	12. b	16. p	20. t	24. q	

True/False Questions

1. F	6. T	11. T	16. F
2. F	7. T	12. F	17. T
3. T	8. F	13. T	18. T
4. F	9. T	14. T	19. F
5. T	10. F	15. F	20. T

Multiple-Choice Questions

1. C	6. B	11. B	16. B
2. F	7. B	12. D	17. C
3. D	8. D	13. B	18. A
4. A	9. C	14. C	19. C
5. E	10. A	15. A	20. B

CHAPTER 12

The Family

Learning Objectives

Following the completion of the study of Chapter 12, you should be able to:

1. Identify three functions of families.

2. Define **family dynamics** and identify some of the factors that influence family dynamics.

3. Provide an example of each of the three ways in which parents influence their children's development through **socialization**.

4. Describe the levels of responsiveness and demandingness that characterize each of Diana Baumrind's four parenting styles: **authoritative parenting, authoritarian parenting, permissive parenting, and rejecting-neglecting (disengaged) parenting**.

5. Discuss the child outcomes associated with the four different parenting styles defined by Baumrind, and the ways in which ethnicity and culture may affect the outcomes associated with the parenting styles.

6. Provide examples of *child* characteristics that influence the bidirectionality of parent–child interactions.

7. Summarize the impact of socioeconomic influences on parenting.

8. Explain the differences in mothers' and fathers' interactions with their children.

9. Discuss several influences on the quality of sibling relationships.

10. Summarize several major changes in family structure in the United States over the past several decades.

11. Identify a number of influences on children's adjustment to parental divorce and remarriage.

12. Using research evidence, compare the child outcomes associated with gay versus heterosexual parents.

13. Discuss several factors that determine the impact of maternal employment on child development.

14. Summarize the recent research on the effects of child care on children's attachment, social behavior, and cognitive and language development.

You Should Know:

Introduction

- what researchers have learned about the relation between family structure and children's development by examining families affected by the one-child policy in China.

The Nature and Functions of the Family *(summary on pg. 457 of text)*

Functions of Families
- what functions of families are common across all societies.

Family Dynamics
- what is meant by family dynamics and what relationships are involved, both within the family and from outside the family.
- what factors affect family dynamics and increase its complexity.
- what the implications of understanding the complexity of family dynamics are for conducting research on families.

Box 12.1: A Closer Look: Parent-Child Relationships in Adolescence
- how parent-child relationships tend to change and how they tend to remain the same as children become adolescents.

The Influence of Parental Socialization *(summary on pg. 466 of text)*

Introduction
- the three ways in which parents can influence their children's development through socialization.

Parenting Styles and Practices
- the dimensions on which parents can differ in terms of their behavior and attitudes that can influence the pattern of parent-child interactions.
- the parenting styles have been identified by Baumrind, including the parenting behaviors and attitudes characteristic of each style, and the common outcomes for children of each style.
- how the outcomes associated with different parenting styles and practices can differ in different subcultures and cultures.

The Child as an Influence on Parenting
- how children's physical attractiveness can influence parental behavior.
- how children's behavior and temperaments may influence parental behavior.
- how the bidirectionality of parent-child interactions can support and maintain parents' and children's behavior.

Socioeconomic Influences on Parenting
- how parents who differ in socioeconomic status differ in parenting style and practices and what beliefs, values, and environmental factors appear to contribute to these differences.
- how economic stress and poverty are related to the quality of parenting and family interactions and how social support can diminish some of these effects.

Box 12.2: A Closer Look: Homelessness
- the likely impact of homelessness on children's and adolescents' adjustment.

Mothers, Fathers, and Siblings *(summary on pg. 471 of text)*

Differences in Mothers' and Fathers' Interactions with Their Children
- how the degree of involvement in parenting and parent-child interactions differ for mothers and fathers and for daughters and sons.

Sibling Relationships
- how siblings can influence one another's development for better and for worse.
- what factors play a role in whether or not siblings get along with one another, as well as what parents can do to increase the likelihood of positive interactions among their children.

Changes in Families in the United States *(summary on pg. 482 of text)*

Introduction
- how the family in the United States has changed during the past 50 years.

Older Parents
- how differences in the resources of younger and older parents relate to differences in their parenting practices.
- how older parents differ from younger parents in their attitudes about parenting.

Box 12.3: Individual Differences: Adolescents as Parents

- what factors increase and decrease the likelihood that teenagers will become parents.

- the apparent consequences of adolescent parenting for the adolescent and the child and what factors mitigate these consequences.

- what factors influence whether the father will be involved and what the consequences of his involvement appear to be for the child.

Divorce

- what the research suggests are the consequences of divorce for children and the likelihood that they will experience significant, enduring problems.

- what factors appear to influence the impact of divorce on children.

- what types of custody arrangements exist and how experts believe these influence children's adjustment.

- how the correlates of divorce compare to the effects of ongoing marital conflict.

Stepparenting

- the characteristics of typical stepparent-child relationships and what appears to influence whether these relationships will be positive or negative.

- how the age and sex of the child and the parenting behaviors of both the custodial parent and the stepparent are related to children's adjustment in stepfamilies.

Lesbian and Gay Parents

- how the parenting of lesbian parents and heterosexual mothers compares.

- how children of gay and lesbian parents compare to children of heterosexual parents.

- how family dynamics appear to influence the adjustment of children of gay and lesbian parents.

Maternal Employment and Child Care *(summary on pg. 490 of text)*

Introduction

- how the employment rate for mothers of children of different ages has changed over the past several decades.

The Effects of Maternal Employment

- how maternal employment when children are infants appears to influence infants' development.

- how maternal employment appears to influence children's development both positively and negatively and the child and parent factors that appear to affect whether the impact is positive or negative.

The Effects of Child Care

- what types of child care are common in the U.S.

- how child care is associated with attachment and the parent-child relationship and how the quality and amount of child care may contribute to this influence.

- how child care is associated with children's social, cognitive, and language development and how the quality and amount of child care may contribute to these associations.

- how and why the correlates of child care can differ for children from low-income families versus children from working and middle class families.

- the characteristics of high-quality child care programs.

Key Term Matching I: Definitions

Instructions: Match each key term with its definition.

KEY TERM

1. _____ survival of offspring

2. _____ rejecting-neglecting parenting

3. _____ authoritative parenting

4. _____ family dynamics

5. _____ socialization

6. _____ parenting styles

7. _____ cultural training

8. _____ authoritarian parenting

9. _____ bidirectionality of parent-child interactions

10. _____ economic function

11. _____ complex stepfamilies

12. _____ permissive parenting

DEFINITION

a. parenting behaviors and attitudes that set the emotional climate of parent-child interactions

b. a function of the family; pertains to providing the means for children to acquire the skills and other resources they need to be economically productive adults

c. the process through which children acquire the values, standards, skills, knowledge, and behaviors that are appropriate for their role in their culture

d. a parenting style that is high in demandingness and low in responsiveness

e. the way in which the family operates as a whole

f. a function of the family; pertains to ensuring that children survive by attending to their needs

g. a parenting style that is high in both demandingness and responsiveness

h. the notion that parents' characteristics and behavior affect children's characteristics and behavior and vice versa

i. a parenting style that is low in demandingness and high in responsiveness

j. a function of the family; pertains to teaching children the basic values in their culture

k. families that contain half siblings or stepsiblings

l. a parenting style that is low in both demandingness and responsiveness

Key Term Matching II: Applications, Examples, and More

Instructions: Match each key term with an application or example of the term.

KEY TERM

1. _____ authoritative parenting
2. _____ economic function
3. _____ rejecting-neglecting parenting
4. _____ family dynamics
5. _____ socialization
6. _____ parenting styles

7. _____ survival of offspring
8. _____ authoritarian parenting
9. _____ cultural training
10. _____ bidirectionality of parent-child interactions
11. _____ permissive parenting
12. _____ complex stepfamilies

APPLICATION OR EXAMPLE

a.   the most fundamental function of the family

b.   parents who exhibit this tend to be focused on their own needs rather than on their children, and their children are at-risk for a host of problem behaviors, including substance abuse, internalizing problems, and promiscuous sexual behavior

c.   in the U.S., this family function would involve teaching children to share and to not hurt other children

d.   one way parents accomplish this is by providing and controlling their children's opportunities, such as signing up their daughters for ballet lessons but not for the local soccer team

e.   this notion emphasizes that no family member functions in isolation and that all members are interdependent and reciprocally influence one another

f.   this phenomenon would be demonstrated by a study showing that colic in early infancy causes poor parental responsiveness in late infancy, which in turn causes poor self-regulation in toddlerhood

g.   parents who exhibit this set clear limits for their children but allow their children considerable autonomy within these limits

h.   adolescents have a particularly hard time in families of this type

i.   although parents who exhibit this can be very affectionate, they do not require their children to behave in appropriate ways and thus would be relatively unlikely to intervene if their children hit and kick them in the midst of a temper tantrum

j.   even though parents who exhibit this are likely to use threats and punishment if children do poorly at school, their children tend to be relatively low in academic competence

k.   parental responsiveness and demandingness are two facets of these

l.   sending children to school in the U.S. and teaching children how to weave baskets to sell in Columbia are examples of this family function

True/False Questions

Instructions: Indicate whether each item is true or false.

_____ 1. Family dynamics involves the relationships within the family and thus is not concerned with hereditary characteristics.

_____ 2. Permissive parents expect children to comply with their demands without question or explanation.

_____ 3. Rejecting-neglecting parents are focused on their own needs rather than on their children's needs.

_____ 4. Although authoritarian parenting appears to be associated with negative outcomes for African-American adolescent girls, it appears to be associated with positive outcomes for Euro-American adolescent girls.

_____ 5. Chinese children's views of parental strictness as being a sign of parental involvement may explain why parental control has few negative effects on Chinese-American children.

_____ 6. Although fathers show differential treatment to attractive and unattractive infants, mothers appear to be able to disregard the attractiveness of their infants and treat attractive and unattractive infants the same.

_____ 7. Children's behavior with their parents can be influenced by the children's perceptions of their parents' attitudes toward them.

_____ 8. The bidirectionality of parent-child interactions implies that parents can both influence their children's behavior and be influenced by their children's behavior.

_____ 9. SES differences in parenting style may reflect differences in the environments in which families live.

_____ 10. The amount of time parents spend playing with their children is fairly comparable across a wide variety of cultures.

_____ 11. Siblings with similar temperaments tend to get along better than siblings with different temperaments, even when the similar temperaments are both difficult.

_____ 12. In the United States in 2003, the proportions of Latino and African-American children living with two married parents were equal to the proportion of Euro-American children living with two married parents

_____ 13. On measures of adjustment ranging from maternal stress to financial resources to positivity in parenting, older parents do better than parents in their early 20s.

_____ 14. It appears that the risk associated with being the child of an adolescent mother is due to a greater degree to the quality of the home environment and the quality of parenting and to a lesser degree to the adolescents' age.

_____   15.   The level of parental conflict may predict outcomes for children more than the divorce itself.

_____   16.   The frequency of children's contact with their noncustodial parent following divorce is an important factor in predicting children's adjustment.

_____   17.   Stepparents who attempt to develop their own role as disciplinarian, independent of the custodial parent, tend to integrate themselves into families with greater ease than do other stepparents.

_____   18.   Lesbian mothers appear to emphasize self-control in their children to a lesser extent than do heterosexual mothers.

_____   19.   In two-parent families, maternal employment is associated with decreased father involvement.

_____   20.   When nonmaternal child care has been shown to have effects on attachment, the effects have been large in magnitude.

Multiple-Choice Questions

1. Family dynamics includes the influence of which of the following?
   A. parents on children
   B. children on parents
   C. siblings on each other
   D. mother and father on each other
   E. all of the above

2. Which of the following is an example of a parent's direct socialization of modesty?
   A. Abigail (the mother) dresses in reserved clothing.
   B. Judith signs her child up for a class at the local church on growing up with religion.
   C. Jonathon explains to his child how important it is to have respect for oneself and one's appearance.
   D. All of the above are examples of a parent's direct socialization of modesty.

3. Parents who are high in warmth and low in control are considered to exhibit which of the following parenting styles?
   A. permissive
   B. authoritative
   C. rejecting-neglecting
   D. authoritarian

4. Authoritative parents are those who:
   A. are abusive.
   B. are highly demanding and unresponsive.
   C. have little interest in disciplining their children.
   D. are attentive, communicative, and consistent in their discipline.

5. Children of which type of parents tend to be low in academic competence and high in impulsive or antisocial behavior (e.g., aggression, drug use)?
   A. permissive
   B. authoritative
   C. rejecting-neglecting
   D. authoritarian
   E. both A and C
   F. both A and D
   G. both C and D

6. Which of the following is NOT an example of psychological control?
   A. discounting children's feelings
   B. withdrawing love and attention when children behave poorly
   C. threatening children with physical punishment for noncompliance
   D. belittling children's worth

7. Bidirectionality of parent-child interactions refers to the finding that:
   A. children learn to communicate from the reciprocity of early parent-infant babbling.
   B. children's behavior affects parents' behavior, which in turn affects children's behavior.
   C. parents' and children's ethnicity affects their interactions with each other.
   D. parents' genotypes influence both parents' phenotypes and children's genotypes.

8. Imagine that researchers interested in the bidirectional influence of children's compliance with parental requests and parental use of reasoning examined these two variables when a group of children was at each of three ages: two years old, five years old, and eight years old. Which of the following would be the best support for the bidirectional influence of these variables?
   A. Greater compliance at age two was associated with greater reasoning at age five, which was associated with greater compliance at age eight.
   B. Greater reasoning at age two was associated with less compliance at age five, which was associated with less compliance at age eight.
   C. Greater reasoning at age two was associated with greater reasoning at age five, which was associated with greater compliance at age eight.
   D. Greater compliance at age two was associated with greater compliance at age five, which was associated with greater reasoning at age eight.
   E. All of the above would be support for the bidirectional influence of these variables.

9. Which of the following is a true statement about the association between SES and mother-child communication?
   A. Higher-SES mothers talk more with their children than do lower-SES mothers.
   B. Lower-SES mothers talk more with their children than do higher-SES mothers.
   C. Lower-SES mothers elicit more talk from their children than do higher-SES mothers.
   D. Higher-SES mothers and lower SES mothers do not differ in the amount they talk to their children.

10. Compared to parents with less education, parents with more education are more likely to:
    A. view children as active participants in their own development.
    B. allow children to voice opinions about rules and discipline.
    C. be concerned with their children' thoughts and feelings.
    D. do all of the above.
    E. do none of the above.

11. In Western industrialized cultures, fathers' play with their children is more likely than mothers' play to include:
    A. reading.
    B. rough-and-tumble play.
    C. teaching.
    D. playing with toys indoors.
    E. all of the above.
    F. none of the above.

12. Which of the following does NOT increase the likelihood that siblings will get along?
    A. similarity of siblings' temperaments
    B. preparation of older siblings for the arrival of a new sibling
    C. similar treatment by parents
    D. high-quality parental relationship
    E. All of the above do increase the likelihood that siblings will get along.

13. Compared to younger mothers, older mothers:
    A. are less satisfied with their role as parents.
    B. have more financial resources.
    C. display less positive emotion with their babies.
    D. experience more stress.

14. All of the following increase the likelihood that children will experience negative consequences from their parents' divorce EXCEPT:
    A. noncustodial parent authoritative style
    B. custodial parent isolation from social support
    C. custodial parent authoritarian style
    D. conflict between parents

15. In which of the following age groups are youth most likely to blame themselves for divorce?
    A. younger children
    B. older children
    C. young adolescents
    D. older adolescents

16. Which of the following is a true statement about children and stepfathers?
   A. Relationships between children and stepfathers tend to be particularly bad in simple stepfamilies.
   B. Conflict between children and biological fathers is more common than conflict between children and stepfathers.
   C. Over time, stepfathers tend to become emotionally distant and disengaged parents.
   D. Stepchildren do not tend to contribute to the conflict with their stepfathers.

17. Which of the following is a true statement about the adjustment of children of gay and lesbian parents?
   A. The factors involved in adjustment tend to be quite different from the factors involved in the adjustment of children of heterosexual parents.
   B. The adjustment of children of lesbian parents does not appear to be associated with the extent to which the mother and her partner share child-care duties.
   C. Children of lesbian parents tend to be teased more than other children.
   D. The adjustment of the sons of gay men appears to be associated with the inclusion of the father's partner in family life.

18. Which of the following is a true statement about the effects of maternal employment on infants?
   A. There is little evidence that maternal employment has a negative influence on infants.
   B. Part-time maternal employment tends to be worse for infants than full-time maternal employment.
   C. The effects of maternal employment on infants appear to be particularly pronounced for infants whose mothers are not sensitive caregivers.
   D. The effects of maternal employment on infants appear to be limited to infants' social development.

19. The large-scale study of the effects of child care that was funded by the National Institute of Child Health and Development has demonstrated that which of the following is the most important predictor of how children in nonmaternal care fare?
   A. quality of child care
   B. stability of child care
   C. family characteristics
   D. age at which child care began

20. The large-scale study of the effects of child care that was funded by the National Institute of Child Health and Development demonstrated that which of the following child care characteristics was a critical predictor of behavioral problems in children from working and middle class families?

A. quality of child care
B. amount of child care
C. number of changes in caregivers
D. both quality and amount of child care
E. both quality of child care and number of changes in caregivers
F. both amount of child care and number of changes in caregivers
G. quality of child care, amount of child care, and number of changes in caregivers

Essay Questions

Instructions: Answer the following essay questions on a separate sheet of paper.

1. Describe the family dynamics that may be involved when the mother in the Smith family, made up of a mother and a father and their two young children--Fiona, who is one year old and Gavin, who is three years old--decides to go back to school part time. When the mother is at school two days a week, the children's paternal grandmother (their father's mother) will take care of them. What are some possible effects on how the family operates as a whole, and how might it affect the development of the two children in the family?

2. Describe the child development outcomes that are associated with an authoritarian parenting style and a permissive parenting style. Why do you think each of these parenting styles is associated with these particular outcomes for children?

3. Describe the influences of poverty and homelessness on parenting styles and behaviors. Are any of the parental behaviors that are more common for these children than for other children beneficial for children living in these circumstances? Why or why not?

4. How do you think parents influence children's relationships with their siblings? Be specific and provide supportive examples.

5. What advice can you give to custodial parents and stepparents to increase the likelihood of children adjusting well to living with a stepparent?

Answer Key

Key Term Matching I

1. f	3. g	5. c	7. j	9. h	11. k
2. l	4. e	6. a	8. d	10. b	12. i

Key Term Matching II

1. g	3. b	5. d	7. a	9. c	11. i
2. l	4. e	6. k	8. j	10. f	12. h

True/False Questions

1. F	6. F	11. F	16. F
2. F	7. T	12. F	17. F
3. T	8. T	13. T	18. T
4. F	9. T	14. T	19. F
5. T	10. F	15. T	20. F

Multiple-Choice Questions

1. E	6. C	11. B	16. C
2. C	7. B	12. E	17. D
3. A	8. A	13. B	18. C
4. D	9. A	14. A	19. C
5. E	10. D	15. A	20. F

CHAPTER 13

Peer Relationships

Learning Objectives

Following the completion of the study of Chapter 13, you should be able to:

1. Explain the unique contributions that **peers** make to development.

2. Compare preschool children's interactions with friends and with non-friends.

3. Summarize the developmental changes that occur in friendships between the early school years and adolescence.

4. Identify differences and similarities in the functions that friendships fulfill among boys and girls.

5. List the factors that predict friendship formation among children during the preschool and elementary school years.

6. Discuss the changes that occur in children's stable **cliques** from middle childhood through late adolescence.

7. Identify the characteristics of children who are most likely to experience negative influences from peer groups or **gangs**.

8. Explain how a child's **sociometric status** is determined.

9. Compare the characteristics of children in each of the four categories of sociometric status.

10. Describe the near- and long-term risks and negative outcomes associated with having an undesirable peer status.

11. Identify different subcategories of rejected children, and discuss the causes of peer rejection for the children in each subcategory.

12. Based on the material in the text, discuss the child and family characteristics that are associated with popularity in children.

13. Provide examples of the ways that parents contribute to their children's relationships as gatekeepers, as coaches, and as models.

14. Identify aspects of the sociometric context that are important in children's peer relationships.

You Should Know:

Introduction

- what observations Anna Freud and Sophie Dann made of a group of children whose parents had been killed by Hitler and what their conclusions about the importance of peer relationships were.

- what research conducted by Suomi and Harlow demonstrated and how some of their findings with socially isolated monkeys supported Freud's and Dann's observations of children.

What is Special About Peer Relationships? (*summary on pg. 497 of text*)

- what Piaget, Vygotsky, and Sullivan believed was unique to peer relationships and the ways in which peer relationships facilitate children's development.

Friendships (*summary on pg. 507 of text*)

Introduction
- how friendships differ from other peer relationships.

Early Peer Interactions and Friendships
- what evidence supports the existence of friendships in very young children.
- how young children's behavior differs when they are interacting with friends versus nonfriends.

Developmental Changes in Friendship
- how school-age children's behavior differs when they are interacting with friends versus nonfriends.
- how children's conceptions of what a friend is and what is important in a friendship changes from childhood through early adolescence and adolescence.
- what researchers and theorists have claimed accounts for these developmental changes in children's friendship conceptions.

The Functions of Friendships
- how friendships can provide emotional support and understanding for children and how they appear to provide a buffer for children during difficult times.
- how friendships can provide a context for the development of social and cognitive skills.

- how the features of friendships appear to differ between the friendships of girls and those of boys.

Effects of Friendships on Psychological Functioning and Behavior over Time

- what long-term benefits appear to be associated with having friends and why it is difficult to determine the direction of causality.

- how children's aggression and use of alcohol and drugs are associated with the aggression and alcohol and drug use displayed by their friends and why it is difficult to determine the direction of causality.

- which children and adolescents may be most susceptible to the negative influence of friends.

Children's Choice of Friends

- what factors appear to influence with which of their peers children become friends and how these factors change with development.

Box 13.1: Individual Differences: Culture and Children's Peer Experience

- how cultural differences in values, expectations, and the structure of society appear to influence the quantity and types of children's interactions with peers.

Peers in Groups (*summary on pg. 512 of text*)

The Nature of Young Children's Groups

- that dominance hierarchies exist even within groups of very young children.

Cliques and Social Networks in Middle Childhood and Early Adolescence

- the features and functions of school-age children's cliques.

Cliques and Social Networks in Adolescence

- how the structure and dynamics of cliques change as children enter preadolescence and develop through adolescence.

- what crowds are and how they may influence adolescents' peer interactions and behaviors.

Boys and Girls in Cliques and Crowds

- how boys' and girls' clique affiliations differ.

Negative Influences of Cliques and Social Networks

- how the members of a clique or larger social network may influence each others' behaviors in negative ways.

- what features of gangs are common and how gang membership appears to influence adolescents' and young adults' behavior.

- how family and cultural influences appear to play a role in the potential for peer-group promotion of problem behavior.

Box 3.2: A Closer Look: Romantic Relationships With Peers

- the developmental pattern of mixed-sex peer relationships.

- how adolescents' romantic relationships are associated with adjustment and with other personal relationships.

Status in the Peer Group *(summary on pg. 523 of text)*

Introduction

- why sociometric status is considered important by developmental researchers.

Measurement of Peer Status

- how sociometric status is generally measured by researchers.

Characteristics Associated with Sociometric Status

- what factors appear to play a role in how well-liked a child is.

- how children are classified as popular, rejected, neglected, average, and controversial.

- what characteristics and behaviors are common to children in each status group.

- how being perceived as popular by the peer group differs from being sociometrically popular.

- what types of rejected children exist and whether aggressive behavior and withdrawn behavior are always associated with rejection.

Box 13.3: Fostering Children's Peer Acceptance

- what social skills training is and upon what assumption it relies.

- what features are common to social skills training programs.

- the extent to which these intervention programs have been successful.

Stability of Sociometric Status

- the extent to which sociometric status is stable over time and how stability is related to the time period and the status group of interest.

Developmental Trends in Predictors of Children's Sociometric Status

- how the characteristics of popular children change with age.

- how the apparent influence of aggressive and withdrawn behavior on sociometric status changes with age.

Cross-Cultural Similarities and Differences in Factors Related to Peer Status
- what similarities and differences in the behaviors related to peer status have been found cross-culturally and what may account for cultural differences.

Peer Status as a Predictor of Risk
- how peer status is associated with academic performance and long-term adjustment.
- how social withdrawal and victimization are associated with later adjustment.
- the extent to which we can conclude that a causal path exists between rejection and poor long-term adjustment.

The Role of Parents in Children's Peer Relationships *(summary on pg. 527 of text)*

Relations Between Attachment and Competence with Peers
- the perspective of attachment theorists on the association between parent-child attachment and peer relationships.
- what evidence supports these theoretical views and why this link may exist.

Quality of Ongoing Parent-Child Interactions and Peer Relationships
- how mothers' and fathers' parenting practices are associated with children's peer relationships and why these associations may exist.
- the extent to which we can conclude the existence of a causal relationship between parent-child interactions and children's peer interactions.

Parental Beliefs and Behaviors
- how parents' beliefs about their children's social behaviors and about their own role in children's social behaviors are associated with children's peer interactions.

Gatekeeping, Coaching, and Modeling by Parents
- how parents may influence children's peer relationships through gatekeeping behaviors and by modeling and coaching socially competent behaviors.

Family Stress and Children's Social Competence
- how family economic status is associated with children's peer relations and what may account for this association.

Key Term Matching I: Definitions

Instructions: Match each key term with its definition.

KEY TERM

1. _____ peers

2. _____ crowds

3. _____ victimized peer status

4. _____ social skills training

5. _____ friendships

6. _____ aggressive-rejected children

7. _____ sociometric status

8. _____ withdrawn-rejected children

9. _____ rejected peer status

10. _____ gangs

11. _____ controversial peer status

12. _____ popular peer status

13. _____ cliques

14. _____ neglected peer status

15. _____ relational aggression

16. _____ reciprocated best friendship

DEFINITION

a. a category of sociometric status that includes children who are not particularly liked or disliked by their peers

b. intimate, reciprocated positive relationships between two people

c. a friendship in which two children view one another as best friends

d. friendship groups that children voluntarily join or form themselves

e. groups of adolescents who have similar stereotyped reputations

f. loosely-organized groups of adolescents or young adults that identify as a group and often engage in illegal activities

g. a category of sociometric status that includes children who are liked by few peers and disliked by many peers

h. a category of sociometric status that includes children who are liked by few peers and disliked by many peers *and* are socially withdrawn and often timid

i. a measurement of the degree to which children are liked or disliked by their peers as a group

j.   a category of sociometric status that includes children who are liked by few peers and disliked by many peers *and* are especially prone to hostile and physically aggressive behavior

k.   a type of aggression that involves trying to hurt the social relationships of others

l.   a category of sociometric status that includes children who are liked by many peers and disliked by few peers

m.   training programs aimed at teaching rejected children the knowledge and skills that are believed to be associated with positive peer relations

n.   individuals who are of the same age and status

o.   a category of sociometric status that includes children who are liked by a number of peers and disliked by a number of other peers

p.   children in this status group tend to be the targets of their peers' aggression and demeaning behavior

Key Term Matching II: Applications, Examples, and More

Instructions: Match each key term with an application or example of the term.

KEY TERM

1. _____ controversial peer status

2. _____ reciprocated best friendship

3. _____ peers

4. _____ social skills training

5. _____ crowds

6. _____ gangs

7. _____ popular peer status

8. _____ withdrawn-rejected children

9. _____ rejected peer status

10. _____ aggressive-rejected children

11. _____ neglected peer status

12. _____ sociometric status

13. _____ cliques

14. _____ relational aggression

15. _____ friendships

APPLICATION OR EXAMPLE

a.   this may involve teaching children strategies they can use in specific peer contexts

b.   children in this status group tend to have trouble finding constructive solutions to difficult social situations

c.   research has indicated that children who are victimized by their peers do better in terms of adjustment if they have this type of friendship

d.   in middle childhood, these tend to include children of the same sex and race

e.   children in this status group tend to be cooperative and friendly and to regulate their emotions well

f.   40% to 50% of rejected children tend to fall into this category

g.   children may be asked to nominate the children whom they like the most and those whom they like the least in order for researchers to calculate a measure of this for each child in the group

h.   "jocks" and "loners" are examples of types of these that are typical among American high school students

i.   some evidence suggests that even very young children have these

j.   adolescents tend to join these for protection

k.   spreading rumors and excluding peers are examples of this

l.   children who are classified as this tend to exhibit withdrawn behavior coupled with negative actions or emotions

m.   theorists such as Piaget, Vygotsky, and Sullivan have argued that children's relationships with _____ provide a unique context for development

n.   children who are classified as this tend to be both less sociable and less aggressive than average children, but they display relatively few behaviors that differentiate them from other children

o.   children who are classified as this tend to exhibit characteristics of both popular and rejected children

True/False Questions

Instructions: Indicate whether each item is true or false.

_____ 1. Starting in the second year of life, children begin to show preferences for some peers over others.

_____ 2. During the school years (ages 9 and 10), children are likely to define best friends primarily as peers with whom they play all the time.

_____ 3. Adolescents generally view their friends as being untrustworthy.

_____ 4. Girls' best friendships tend to be more fragile and of shorter duration than boys' best friendships.

_____ 5. Boys who are nonaggressive and nondisruptive appear to be easily influenced by disruptive and aggressive friends.

_____ 6. Friends who are depressed tend to foster resiliency in their close friends, as ruminating about problems in friendships appears to help buffer children from negative feelings.

_____ 7. The turnover rate of members of middle childhood cliques has been shown to be approximately 50% over eight months.

_____ 8. Older adolescents tend to be particularly concerned with conforming to their peer groups' norms regarding dress and behavior.

_____ 9. Adolescents are more likely to engage in illegal activities if members of their cliques and social groups do so.

_____ 10. College students involved in athletics and fraternities or sororities are more likely than are other students to engage in binge drinking.

_____ 11. Having authoritative, involved parents tends to protect adolescents from peer pressure to use drugs.

_____ 12. Being sociometrically popular has little to do with children's personality or social behavior and is associated almost entirely with physical attractiveness, athleticism, and family socioeconomic status.

_____ 13. Adolescents who are labeled as popular by their peers tend to be those who are low in aggression and high in cooperation.

_____ 14. Socially withdrawal in kindergarten is associated with peer rejection a few years later.

_____ 15. Neglected children tend to exhibit characteristics of both popular and controversial children.

_____ 16. In recent years, some of the correlates of peer acceptance and rejection in China appear to be changing and becoming more similar to the correlates common in Western cultures.

_____   17.   Victimized children tend to be aggressive.

_____   18.   Children who have secure attachments with their caregivers are less likely to seek out positive and rewarding peer relationships than are other children.

_____   19.   Preschool children whose parents coach them on their social interactions are more likely to be socially withdrawn and rejected by their peers than are preschool children whose parents allow them to figure out their own strategies for social interactions.

_____   20.   The quality of adolescents' romantic relationships is associated with the quality of the relationships with their parents and with other peers.

Multiple-Choice Questions

1. Suomi and Harlow's study of isolated monkeys who were then placed with other monkeys demonstrated that:
   A. peer interaction had no impact on the abnormal behaviors of previously isolated monkeys.
   B. peers provided previously isolated monkeys with social interactions, but did not assist them in learning about their environments.
   C. peers provided previously isolated monkeys with significant social and emotional experiences that enabled them to explore their environment and engage in social interactions.
   D. peers alone can produce optimal development in monkeys.

2. As children develop, their friendships:
   A. tend to emphasize closeness and loyalty to a lesser extent.
   B. tend to involve rewards and costs to a greater extent.
   C. are less likely to remain intact following conflict.
   D. all of the above
   E. none of the above

3. Having supportive friends is LEAST likely to be able to help children:
   A. who are experiencing major stressful life experiences.
   B. experience loneliness to a lesser degree.
   C. who are being victimized by their peers.
   D. as they transition to a new school.

4. Which of the following features of friendships tend NOT to differ between the friendships of elementary school boys and the friendships of elementary school girls?
   A. level of help and guidance
   B. level of intimacy
   C. level of companionship and recreational opportunities
   D. difficulty resolving conflict

5. Which of the following does NOT appear to contribute to cultural differences in children's experience with peers?
   A. educational practices
   B. parents' beliefs about independence
   C. parents' expectations for skills of children of different ages
   D. whether the society is kin-based or not
   E. All of the above *do* appear to influence cultural differences in children's experience with peers.

6. Cliques refer to which of the following?
   A. the friendships of preschool children
   B. friendship groups that children voluntarily form or join
   C. groups of children or adolescents with the same stereotyped reputation
   D. groups of adolescents that often engage in illegal activities

7. Which of the following tends to be true of middle childhood friendship cliques?
   A. Members are of the same race.
   B. They include children with great variability on behavioral characteristics.
   C. They include members of both sexes.
   D. All members consider all other members close friends.

8. Which of the following is a true statement about girls' and boys' diversity of friends?
   A. Girls tend to have a *greater* diversity of friends than boys.
   B. Girls tend to have a *less* diversity of friends than boys.
   C. Girls and boys tend to have *similar* diversity of friends.
   D. The diversity of girls' and boys' friends tends to be similar prior to adolescence and then becomes more different.

9. In comparison to adolescents, school-age children:
   A. are more likely to be part of a crowd.
   B. are more likely to belong to multiple cliques.
   C. tend to look more to individual relationships rather than group relationships to fulfill their social needs.
   D. demonstrate all of the above.
   E. demonstrate none of the above.

10. Individuals join and remain in gangs because they provide members with:
    A. a way to spend time.
    B. protection.
    C. a sense of belonging.
    D. all of the above.

11. Which of the following decreases children's likelihood of being negatively influenced by the peer group?
    A. having authoritarian parents
    B. living with a stepfather
    C. being independent from mother
    D. all of the above
    E. none of the above

12. Neglected children are those who:
    A. are rejected.
    B. have low social impact.
    C. have high social impact.
    D. are aggressive.
    E. demonstrate both A and B.
    F. demonstrate both C and D.

13. Which of the following is a true statement about the aggression levels of school-age children who are sociometrically popular?
    A. Popular children rarely exhibit aggressive behavior.
    B. Popular children exhibit levels of aggression similar to those of rejected children.
    C. Popular children differ from sociometrically average children in aggression only in terms of aggression that is hostile and angry in nature.
    D. Popular children differ from sociometrically average children in aggression only in terms of aggression that is assertive (such as pushing to get a toy) in nature.

14. Which of the following is a true statement about predictors of sociometric status across development?
    A. Withdrawn behavior tends to become a less important predictor of peer rejection as children get older.
    B. Overtly aggressive behavior tends to become a more important predictor of peer rejection as children get older.
    C. The predictors of sociometric popularity tend to remain the same across development.
    D. Adolescents who are labeled as popular by their peers tend to exhibit the same behaviors as those who are considered popular by sociometric standards.
    E. All of the above are true statements.

15. Children who are in which of the following categories in third grade are most likely to experience internalizing symptoms when they are in tenth grade?
   A. popular
   B. controversial
   C. average
   D. aggressive-rejected

16. Which of the following is NOT likely to be considered indicative of an internalizing symptom?
   A. delinquency
   B. depression
   C. loneliness
   D. obsessive-compulsive behavior

17. Which of the following is a true statement about the long-term adjustment of withdrawn children?
   A. These children tend not to differ from other children once they become adults.
   B. Withdrawn girls, but not boys, tend to have poor long-term adjustment.
   C. Withdrawn boys, but not girls, tend to have poor long-term adjustment.
   D. Both withdrawn boys and withdrawn girls tend to have poor long-term adjustment.

18. Attachment theorists propose that securely attached children will have high quality peer relationships because these children:
   A. have positive social expectations.
   B. tend to be confident and emotionally positive.
   C. understand relationship reciprocity.
   D. do all of the above.

19. Betsy is a child who has many social difficulties. When she displays aggressive behavior with a peer, her mother is relatively likely to:
   A. believe she should teach Betsy how to handle difficult social situations.
   B. try to organize more opportunities for Betsy to have interaction with peers.
   C. believe the aggressive behavior is part of Betsy's nature.
   D. believe it would be easy to stop Betsy from being aggressive in the future.

20. Which of the following may account for the association between family economic status and children's peer relations?
   A. parental warmth
   B. parental monitoring
   C. prejudice
   D. all of the above

Essay Questions

Instructions: Answer the following essay questions on a separate sheet of paper.

1. Do preschool friends have more or less conflict than preschool nonfriends? Describe how the ways that conflict gets resolved differ between those who are friends and those who are nonfriends.

2. Do you think social interactions, including friendships and associations with cliques, are more important to adolescent boys or girls, or are they equally important to adolescents of both sexes? Give examples to support your view.

3. Does researchers' classification of children into the five basic acceptance categories seem accurate to you? Can you think of children you knew growing up who could have been placed into each of these categories? If so, give examples. If not, explain why you cannot place anyone into a particular category. Additionally, do you think any categories are inaccurate or would you add any other categories?

4. Describe the ways in which parents can influence their children's peer interactions through the following three processes: (1) gatekeeping, (2) coaching, and (3) modeling. Be sure to give an example of each. To what extent do you think the influence of these parental behaviors changes with the age of the child?

5. Imagine a school-age child who is having trouble with her peers. She is poorly liked by them, and she has few friends. Which of these two issues do you think is more serious? Why? Be sure to describe the negative outcomes associated with being rejected and with having few or no friends as well as the positive outcomes associated with positive peer relationships.

Answer Key

Key Term Matching I

1. n	4. m	7. i	10. f	13. d	16. c
2. e	5. b	8. h	11. o	14. a
3. p	6. j	9. g	12. l	15. k

Key Term Matching II

1. o	4. a	7. e	10. f	13. d
2. c	5. h	8. l	11. n	14. k
3. m	6. j	9. b	12. g	15. i

True/False Questions

1. T	6. F	11. T	16. T
2. F	7. T	12. F	17. T
3. F	8. F	13. F	18. F
4. T	9. T	14. F	19. F
5. F	10. T	15. F	20. T

Multiple-Choice Questions

1. C	6. B	11. E	16. A
2. E	7. A	12. B	17. C
3. A	8. B	13. C	18. D
4. C	9. E	14. C	19. C
5. E	10. D	15. D	20. D

CHAPTER 14

Moral Development

Learning Objectives

Following the completion of the study of Chapter 14, you should be able to:

1. Explain the differences between the stage of the **morality of constraint** and the stage of **autonomous morality** in Piaget's theory of moral judgment.

2. Identify similarities in Piaget's and Kohlberg's theories of moral judgments with regard to assumptions, methods, and central constructs.

3. Discuss the differences between Kohlberg's **preconventional**, **conventional**, and **postconventional** (or principled) levels of moral judgment.

4. Summarize the criticisms of Kohlberg's work.

5. Describe age-related changes in prosocial moral reasoning as studied by Eisenberg.

6. Provide examples of **moral judgments**, **social conventional judgments**, and **personal judgments**.

7. Identify several factors that affect the development of **conscience**.

8. Summarize the expected age-related changes that characterize the development of **prosocial behavior**.

9. Describe the specific socialization practices within the family, including modeling and communication of values, opportunities for prosocial activities, and discipline and parenting style, that are linked to prosocial moral development.

10. Summarize the changes in aggression that occur between the preschool years and adolescence for children of each gender.

11. Explain the distinction between **instrumental aggression** and **reactive aggression**.

12. Identify several characteristics of aggressive-antisocial children and adolescents.

13. Discuss the following contributors to the development of aggression in children: genetic makeup, socialization by family members, the influence of peers, and cultural factors. Consider the relative significance of each; the specific components of the contributors that are most clearly associated with aggression in children; and the interrelationships among these factors.

14. Explain why it is very difficult to separate out the specific aspects of biology and socialization that affect the development of children's antisocial behavior.

You Should Know:

Moral Judgment (*summary on pg. 544 of text*)

Introduction
- why theorists and researchers have emphasized the reasoning behind a behavior as being critical for determining its morality.

Piaget's Theory of Moral Judgment
- how Piaget studied children's moral development.
- what stages Piaget believed children undergo in the development of morality and what factors he believed contribute to their beliefs in each stage and their advancement from one stage to the next.
- the strengths and weaknesses of Piaget's theory of moral judgment.

Kohlberg's Theory of Moral Judgment
- how Kohlberg examined children's moral development.
- what stages Kohlberg believed individuals undergo in the development of morality, including what types of responses to his moral dilemmas are characteristic of each stage.
- how cognitive development is associated with moral reasoning.
- what major criticisms of Kohlberg's theory have been asserted and what evidence exists to support these criticisms.
- how moral judgment is associated with moral behavior.

Prosocial Moral Judgment
- what types of dilemmas involve prosocial moral judgment.
- what stages of prosocial moral development have been proposed by Eisenberg and how these stages relate to Kohlberg's stages.
- the extent to which the existence of these stages has been supported by research and how cultural differences are believed to influence prosocial moral reasoning.

Domains of Social Judgment
- what types of social judgment exist and when children differentiate among the three domains.

- how cultural and subcultural differences are related to what domain individuals believe particular decisions belong.

The Early Development of Conscience *(summary on pg. 546 of text)*

Introduction

- what the conscience is and how it influences behavior.

Factors Affecting the Development of Conscience

- how parental discipline practices appear to influence the development of children's conscience.
- how individual differences in children are associated with the manner in which children develop a conscience.

Prosocial Behavior *(summary on pg. 555 of text)*

Introduction

- the extent to which prosocial behavior is consistent from childhood into adulthood.

The Development of Prosocial Behavior

- what empathy and sympathy are and how they are relevant to prosocial behavior.
- what factors appear to contribute to children's experiences of empathy and sympathy.
- how prosocial behavior generally develops and what appears to account for this progression.

The Origins of Individual Differences in Prosocial Behavior

- how biological factors likely influence prosocial behavior.
- how parents socialize prosocial behavior and the apparent effectiveness of each manner of socialization.

Box 14.1: A Closer Look: Cultural Contributions to Children's Prosocial and Antisocial Tendencies

- how cultural values and practices are related to children's prosocial and antisocial behaviors.

Box 14.2: Applications: School-Based Interventions for Promoting Prosocial Behavior

- how the Child Development Project attempted to promote prosocial behavior and how effective it was.
- how caring school community programs have influenced children.

Antisocial Behavior (*summary on pg. 567 of text*)

The Development of Aggression and Other Antisocial Behaviors
- how aggression, in terms of quantity, type, and motives, develops during childhood.

Box 14.3: A Closer Look: Oppositional Defiant Disorder and Conduct Disorder
- the characteristics of oppositional defiant disorders and conduct disorders and what factors relate to the development of these disorders.

Consistency of Aggressive and Antisocial Behavior
- the extent to which aggressive and antisocial behavior are consistent over time.
- how juvenile delinquency relates to long-term aggression.
- the association between family risk factors and conduct problems.

Characteristics of Aggressive-Antisocial Children and Adolescents
- what temperamental and personality characteristics are associated with aggression and antisocial behavior.
- how social cognitive factors are associated with aggression and antisocial behavior.

The Origins of Aggression
- how biological factors, family dynamics, and socioeconomic factors appear to contribute to aggression.
- how parenting practices may contribute to aggression and how these associations differ across subcultural groups.
- how friends, the larger peer group, and gangs appear to influence aggressive and antisocial behavior.

Biology and Socialization: Their Joint Influence on Children's Antisocial Behavior
- how biology and socialization appear to interact to contribute to children's aggressive and antisocial behavior.

Box 14.4: Applications: The Fast Track Intervention
- the objectives and methodology of the Fast Track Intervention project.
- the extent to which the program has been successful.

Key Term Matching I: Definitions

Instructions: Match each key term with its definition.

KEY TERM

1. _____ empathy

2. _____ proactive aggression

3. _____ prosocial behavior

4. _____ aggression

5. _____ moral judgments

6. _____ altruistic motives

7. _____ social conventional judgments

8. _____ relational aggression

9. _____ personal judgments

10. _____ instrumental aggression

11. _____ sympathy

12. _____ reactive aggression

13. _____ conscience

DEFINITION

a.   voluntary behavior intended to benefit another

b.   decisions that involve issues of right and wrong, fairness, and justice

c.   unemotional aggression aimed at fulfilling a need or desire

d.   decisions in which individual preferences are the main consideration

e.   emotionally driven, antagonistic aggression

f.   aggression motivated by the desire to obtain a concrete goal

g.   an emotional reaction to another person's emotional state that is highly consistent with that other person's emotional state

h.   the feeling of concern for another person in reaction to that person's emotional state

i.   behavior aimed at hurting or injuring others

j.   reasons for which individuals help others, including empathy, sympathy, and the desire to act in ways that are consistent with one's conscience and moral standards

k.   aggression that harms others by damaging their relationships with peers

l.   an internal regulatory mechanism that increases an individual's ability to conform with standards of behavior that are considered acceptable in his or her culture

m.   decisions that involve customs or regulations intended to ensure social coordination and social organization

Key Term Matching II: Applications, Examples, and More

Instructions: Match each key term with an application or example of the term.

KEY TERM

1. _____ sympathy
2. _____ relational aggression
3. _____ empathy
4. _____ personal judgments
5. _____ conscience
6. _____ altruistic motives
7. _____ social conventional judgments

8. _____ prosocial behavior
9. _____ proactive aggression
10. _____ instrumental aggression
11. _____ moral judgments
12. _____ reactive aggression
13. _____ aggression

APPLICATION OR EXAMPLE

a.   this can promote prosocial behavior by causing a child to feel guilty when he or she engages in unkind behavior

b.   even young children understand that transgressions in these types of decisions are wrong even if an adult says they are acceptable

c.   parents want children to help others as a result of these rather than as a result of a desire to avoid getting in trouble with parents

d.   young children's aggression is generally of this type, as when they push a child so that they can play with a toy they desire

e.   examples of this include helping, sharing, and comforting others

f.   examples of these include decisions about manners and modes of dress in particular contexts

g.   children prone to this are particularly likely to perceive others as possessing hostile motives

h.   a child who is worried about another child who is crying is experiencing this

i.   this evolves from being almost entirely physical in the early years to involving more verbal forms as children develop

j.   adolescents and parents often argue over the issue of whether parents should have any control over these types of decisions

k.   examples of this include spreading negative rumors and excluding a child from a play group

l.   a child who feels sad when she sees another child crying is experiencing this

m.   children prone to this tend to anticipate relatively positive social consequences to their aggression

True/False Questions

Instructions: Indicate whether each item is true or false.

_____ 1. Piaget and Kohlberg agreed that the reasoning behind children's moral judgments is more important than the judgments themselves.

_____ 2. Piaget's morality of constraint stage is most common for children in the concrete operations stage.

_____ 3. There is a modest degree of association between individuals' moral reasoning and how moral their behavior is.

_____ 4. There is little evidence that males and females score differently on Kohlberg's stages of moral judgment.

_____ 5. By late adolescence, the majority of individuals' prosocial moral judgments reflect internalized values.

_____ 6. Children tend to differentiate between moral and social conventional issues beginning in middle childhood.

_____ 7. Toddlers who are temperamentally fearful tend to have a delayed development of conscience.

_____ 8. Empathy is the feeling of concern for another person in reaction to the other's emotional state or condition.

_____ 9. Toddlers do not regularly act in prosocial ways.

_____ 10. There appears to be a genetic component to empathy, sympathy, and prosocial behavior.

_____ 11. Mandatory school-based service activities appear to have no association with later volunteer service.

_____ 12. In the United States, nearly one-quarter of robbery arrests involve juveniles under age 18.

_____ 13. Not all aggression is meant to harm others.

_____ 14. Aggression in young children tends to be relational.

_____ 15. Adolescents who develop conduct problems often come from families in which the mother was single at the time of the adolescent's birth.

_____ 16. Aggressive children are more likely than nonaggressive children to interpret others' ambiguous behavior as being hostile.

_____ 17. Neurological deficits appear to contribute to aggression and antisocial behavior.

_____ 18. The relation between parental abuse and antisocial behavior can be attributed nearly entirely to the genetic links between parent and child.

_____   19.   When families escape from poverty, their young children tend to become less antisocial.

_____   20.   The proportion of female gang members is decreasing.

Multiple-Choice Questions

1. With which of the following statements about morality would cognitive-developmental theorists DISAGREE?
   A. Children actively think about right and wrong.
   B. Social interactions influence children's moral behavior.
   C. A child's moral reasoning changes as a function of cognitive advances.
   D. Children generally learn to behave morally by modeling their parents' behavior.

2. According to Piaget, which of the following is a key factor in children's transition from the morality of constraint to autonomous morality?
   A. parents' requirement for children not to question their rules
   B. the increasing time children spend with peers
   C. children's cognitive immaturity
   D. adults' instructions on the morality and immorality of particular behaviors

3. Which of the following aspects of Piaget's theory of moral reasoning has NOT been supported by empirical research?
   A. Children whose parents are punitive will make progress in moral reasoning more slowly.
   B. Children's cognitive development plays a role in maturity of moral reasoning.
   C. The amount of time children spend with peers influences the maturity of their moral reasoning.
   D. Older children use intentions and motives to a greater extent than do younger children when determining the morality of a behavior.

4. According to Kohlberg, individuals at the least advanced stage of moral reasoning believe that morally right behavior involves:
   A. upholding laws.
   B. universal principles of justice.
   C. obedience to authorities.
   D. doing what is expected by people close to the individual.

5. Which of the following statements constitutes *preconventional* moral reasoning?
   A. "I shouldn't do that because it is my responsibility to fulfill my duties."
   B. "I shouldn't do that because I will get caught and I don't want to be punished."
   C. "I shouldn't do that because it is not in the best interest of society."
   D. "I shouldn't do that because my parents won't think I am a good boy."

6. Imagine the following prosocial moral dilemma: "On his way to school, a boy named Freddie sees another boy fall in the mud and start to cry. The boy says he hurt himself and asks Freddie to help him up, but Freddie is worried that if he helps him, he will get himself all muddy. What should Freddie do?" Which of the following responses would be considered by Eisenberg to be the *most* advanced?
   A. "Freddie should help because the boy is hurt."
   B. "Freddie should not help because his teacher will think he is bad if he gets to school all dirty."
   C. "Freddie should help because he will feel bad if the boy is hurt and he doesn't help him."
   D. "Freddie should not help the boy because he will get dirty, and he doesn't want to get dirty."

7. Which of the following would be considered by most people in Western cultures to be a moral judgment?
   A. choosing whether or not to wear a tie to a formal restaurant
   B. deciding whether to play soccer or baseball after school
   C. deciding whether to put one's napkin on one's lap or leave it on the table
   D. choosing whether or not to return a $10 bill dropped by a person standing ahead in line

8. Which of the following is a true statement about the domains of social judgment in different cultures?
   A. The distinctions among the three domains in terms of what decisions fall into each category are consistent across cultures.
   B. People in different cultures vary as to which decisions are believed to fall into each category.
   C. Any differences across cultures in terms of the domains of social judgment are a result of cultural differences in level of education.
   D. People in some cultures do not differentiate among the three domains of social judgment.
   E. Both B and C are true.

9. What should parents pay attention to when disciplining their children if their goal is for their children to internalize parental standards for behavior?
   A. ensuring the discipline is not so harsh as to cause high levels of distress in children who will then tune out their parents' message
   B. ensuring that the discipline is not so gentle as to not sufficiently arouse the child's attention
   C. both A and B
   D. neither A nor B

10. An emotional reaction to another's emotional state that is similar to the other person's emotional state is referred to as:
   A. altruism.
   B. sympathy.
   C. conscience.
   D. empathy.

11. Results of a twin study designed to estimate the contribution of genetic factors to children's concern for others and prosocial behavior demonstrated that genetic factors make what type of contribution?
   A. no contribution
   B. very slight contribution
   C. modest contribution
   D. large contribution

12. What is the best strategy for parents to encourage children to behave in a prosocial manner?
   A. point out the consequences of prosocial actions for others
   B. point out that the child has upset the parent when he or she doesn't help others
   C. tell children that prosocial behaviors are good and nice
   D. both A and C
   E. all of the above

13. Which of the following parenting practices or styles is associated with increased prosocial behavior in children?
   A. encouraging children to sympathize with others
   B. threatening children for failing to behave prosocially
   C. rewarding children for prosocial behavior
   D. both A and C
   E. both B and C

14. Aggression that is motivated by the desire to obtain an object or concrete goal is referred to as:
   A. physical aggression.
   B. relational aggression.
   C. instrumental aggression.
   D. antisocial aggression.

15. Eleven-year-old Adrian displays severe antisocial and aggressive behaviors. He is cruel to animals, steals from his parents, neighbors, and local stores, and he rarely attends school. Based on these behaviors, Adrian is MOST likely to be diagnosed with:
A. conduct disorder.
B. ADHD.
C. antisocial disorder.
D. oppositional defiant disorder.

16. Which of the following is NOT a characteristic exhibited by infants and preschoolers who later exhibit a high degree of aggressive and antisocial behavior?
A. difficult temperament
B. impulsivity
C. demanding of attention
D. irritability
E. None of the above characteristics is exhibited by infants and preschoolers who later exhibit a high degree of aggressive and antisocial behavior.
F. All of the above are characteristics exhibited by infants and preschoolers who later exhibit a high degree of aggressive and antisocial behavior.

17. In terms of their social cognition when faced with a negative social situation, aggressive children differ from nonaggressive children in which of the following?
A. attributions
B. goals
C. behavioral options
D. expectations of the effectiveness of strategies
E. all of the above

18. Which of the following would be the *weakest* evidence for a biological influence on aggression?
A. Testosterone levels are associated with responses to provocation.
B. Twin studies demonstrate that antisocial behavior runs in families.
C. Many children engage in delinquency at around the same age—adolescence.
D. Neurological deficits that affect attention may contribute to antisocial behavior.

19. Which of the following is a true statement about the relation between parents' use of *abusive punishment* and children's antisocial behavior for children of different racial, ethnic, and cultural groups?
    A. Parents' use of abusive punishment *is* associated with children's antisocial behavior, *regardless* of the group in question.
    B. Parents' use of abusive punishment is *not* associated with children's antisocial behavior for *regardless* of the group in question.
    C. Parents' use of abusive punishment is associated with children's antisocial behavior for *minority* children but not for Euro-American children.
    D. Parents' use of abusive punishment is associated with children's antisocial behavior for *Euro-American* children but not for minority children.

20. Which of the following parenting behaviors is NOT associated with increased antisocial behavior in children?
    A. concessions to children's demands
    B. inconsistent punishing
    C. marital violence
    D. high levels of monitoring
    E. A and B
    F. A and D

Essay Questions

Instructions: Answer the following essay questions on a separate sheet of paper.

1. Describe two similarities and two differences between Piaget's and Kohlberg's theories of moral reasoning. Which theory do you agree with to a greater extent, and why?

2. Describe the pattern of developmental changes in children's prosocial moral reasoning. Give examples where necessary.

3. Describe how sociocultural factors may influence children's understanding of and differentiation among moral, social conventional, and personal judgments. Be specific and provide relevant examples.

4. Are young children capable of taking others' perspectives and experiencing empathy and sympathy? Are they able to engage in altruistic behavior? Provide examples to support your position.

5. Describe the association between parental discipline practices and children's antisocial and aggressive behavior. Be sure to describe the factors that are associated with these behaviors in children, as well as the reasoning for why these associations exist.

Answer Key

Key Term Matching I

1. g	3. a	5. b	7. m	9. d	11. h	13. l
2. c	4. i	6. j	8. k	10. f	12. e	

Key Term Matching II

1. h	3. l	5. a	7. f	9. m	11. b	13. i
2. k	4. j	6. c	8. e	10. d	12. g	

True/False Questions

1. T	6. F	11. F	16. T
2. F	7. F	12. T	17. T
3. T	8. F	13. F	18. F
4. T	9. T	14. F	19. T
5. F	10. T	15. F	20. F

Multiple-Choice Questions

1. D	6. C	11. C	16. F
2. B	7. D	12. A	17. E
3. C	8. B	13. A	18. C
4. C	9. C	14. C	19. A
5. B	10. D	15. A	20. D

CHAPTER 15

Gender Development

Learning Objectives

Following the completion of the study of Chapter 15, you should be able to:

1. Specify milestones in the development of gender stereotypes and gender-typed behavior from infancy through the end of elementary school.

2. Summarize the explanation provided by evolutionary psychology for gender differences. Describe evidence consistent with this perspective.

3. Identify sources of gender socialization within the context of the family, the classroom, and the culture as conveyed in the media.

4. With reference to Kohlberg's cognitive developmental theory, explain the three-stage process involved in the development of a mature understanding of gender.

5. Discuss the similarities and differences between **gender schema theory** and the cognitive developmental explanation of the basis of gender.

6. Provide an example of **gender self-socialization**.

7. Explain the possible reasons for and consequences of **gender segregation**, as presented in Maccoby's theory.

8. Discuss the role of physical development in gender differences in behavior during childhood.

9. Compare the performance of male versus female children in different areas of mental functioning.

10. Summarize gender differences in emotional and social behavior in childhood.

11. Give examples of both biological and social influences on gender differences in self-regulation.

12. Explain why girls are more likely than boys to demonstrate relational aggression, whereas boys show higher levels of physical aggression.

13. Compare the rigidity of sex-typing in boys versus girls.

14. Identify aspects of gender development that are more and less resistant to change.

15. Predict a future shift in cultural norms for patterns of gender behavior.

You Should Know:

Introduction

- the characteristics commonly associated with males and the characteristics commonly associated with females.

Development of Gender Knowledge and Gender-typed Behavior (*summary on pg. 576 of text*)

Introduction

- what infants appear to know about gender.

Milestones in Gender Development

- how children's understanding of gender develops during toddlerhood and the preschool years.
- the extent to which gender segregation exists in elementary school and children's understanding of the biological and social bases of gender.

Perspectives on Gender Development (*summary on pg. 588 of text*)

Biological Perspectives

- how researchers who take an evolutionary view explain the existence of sex differences and what evidence exists to support this perspective.
- how researchers who emphasize the biological source of gender differences use sex differences in hormones and brain structure to explain the existence of sex differences and what evidence exists to support this perspective.

Gender Socialization

- how researchers who take social learning perspective explain the relation between sex differences in behaviors, beliefs, and values and observational learning.
- how parents convey messages about gender and how schools influence gender differences with differential treatment of girls and boys.
- how Kohlberg proposed children come to understand gender and how they learn gender-appropriate behaviors.
- what gender schemas are, how they are proposed to develop, and how they are expected to influence children's self-socialization of gender.

- according to Maccoby, what role is played by gender segregation in the development of sex differences.

Box 15.1: Applications: Where are SpongeSally SquarePants and Curious Jane?

- how males and females are differentially treated by the media and what research has examined the impact of this differential treatment on children's gender views and behavior.

Box 15.2: A Closer Look: Gender Identity: More than Socialization and Learning?

- what case studies of children who underwent "gender reassignment" and children who have gender-identity disorder tell us about the influences of biology and socialization on gender identity.

Gender Comparisons (*summary on pg. 602 of text*)

Introduction

- the typical pattern of scores of males and females showing sex differences.

Physical Growth: Infancy through Adolescence

- the extent to which girls and boys differ physically in infancy and childhood.
- the pattern of physical maturation for males and females and how physical and hormonal changes are associated with psychological and behavioral changes

Cognitive Abilities

- what sex differences exist in the domains of general intelligence, verbal abilities, spatial cognition, and mathematical reasoning and potential explanations for these differences.
- what sex differences exist in developmental disorders and mental illness and how these differences appear to have a biological basis.

Social Behavior

- what differences have been observed in emotional expressiveness, compliance, and prosocial and antisocial behavior.
- the extent to which biology is thought to play a role in gender differences in social behavior.
- how parental socialization influences gender differences in social behavior.
- what differences exist in males' and females' use of the different forms of aggression and the role played by cultural norms in determining the levels of aggression exhibited by males and females.

Box 15.3: A Closer Look: Gender Differences in Eye Contact

- the extent to which male and female infants differ in eye contact.

- how parents' behavior and inborn tendencies are thought to influence this gender difference.

Gender Flexibility and Asymmetry

- what differences exist in the extent to which boys and girls are sex-typed and why this may be the case.

- how parents and other adults perceive and treat children who exhibit behavior that is considered to be more appropriate for the opposite gender.

Key Term Matching I: Definitions

Instructions: Match each key term with its definition.

KEY TERM

1. _____ gender stability

2. _____ congenital adrenal hyperplasia

3. _____ body image

4. _____ gender-essentialist statements

5. _____ instrumental

6. _____ gender segregation

7. _____ menarche

8. _____ gender self-socialization

9. _____ gender identity

10. _____ puberty

11. _____ expressive

12. _____ adrenarche

13. _____ gender constancy

14. _____ androgens

15. _____ spermarche

16. _____ gender schemas

DEFINITION

a.   awareness that one is a member of a particular gender category

b.   the understanding that gender is invariant despite superficial changes in appearance

c.   children's tendency to seek out and interact with same-sex peers and to actively avoid opposite-sex peers

d.   characterized by the tendency to take action and be competitive, independent, aggressive, and self-assertive

e.   the onset of the capacity for ejaculation

f.   the maturation of the adrenal glands

g.   hormones that typically occur at higher levels in males than in females

h.   the process through which children's bias to behave in accord with their gender identity causes them to learn more about gender-consistent entities

i.   the onset of menstruation

j.   awareness that gender remains the same across time

k.   the development of the ability to reproduce

l.   organized mental representations, including everything a person knows about gender

m. characterized by the tendency to be emotional, gentle, empathetic, cooperative, and concerned with the needs of others

n. how an individual perceives and feels about his or her physical appearance

o. assertions about males and females that are stated in such a way as to imply that they are and always will be applicable to all members of the gender in question

p. a condition in which the adrenal glands produce high levels of hormones that have androgenlike effects on a girl's body

Key Term Matching II: Applications, Examples, and More

Instructions: Match each key term with an application or example of the term.

KEY TERM

1. _____ gender schemas

2. _____ menarche

3. _____ expressive

4. _____ gender constancy

5. _____ body image

6. _____ gender identity

7. _____ puberty

8. _____ instrumental

9. _____ androgens

10. _____ adrenarche

11. _____ gender stability

12. _____ gender-essentialist statements

13. _____ gender self-socialization

14. _____ congenital adrenal hyperplasia

15. _____ gender segregation

APPLICATION OR EXAMPLE

a.   this process accounts for young girls acquiring greater knowledge about dolls and kitchen sets than about trucks and construction sets

b.   these are associated with levels of rough-and-tumble play in boys

c.   "Boys don't cry," and "Girls like pink," are examples of these

d.   this is the second stage of Kohlberg's cognitive developmental theory of sex-role development

e.   these include children's memories of interactions with males and females and gender stereotypes transmitted by adults, peers, and the media

f.   perhaps because of the increase in body fat, this is more likely to be negative in teenage girls than in their male peers

g.   across cultures, males tend to considered to be this

h.   in this stage of gender development, children understand that if a boy puts on a dress, he is still a boy

i.   the onset of sexual attraction coincides with this

j.   this is triggered in part by the increase in body fat that is typical of his age

k.   across cultures, females tend to considered to be this

l.   young children establish this by about 30 months

m.   Maccoby proposed that this stems mostly from the different interaction styles of boys and girls

n.   girls with this condition show higher levels of rough-and-tumble play than do other girls

o.   this is accompanied by a growth spurt in height and weight for both boys and girls

True/False Questions

Instructions: Indicate whether each item is true or false.

_____ 1. By six to nine months of age, infants are able to distinguish males and females.

_____ 2. Although gender segregation is shown by children in the United States, it is uncommon in many parts of the world.

_____ 3. According to the evolutionary perspective, females' greater impulse control served an adaptive function.

_____ 4. Girls with congenital adrenal hyperplasia show relatively high levels of pretend play.

_____ 5. Social learning theory is not concerned with differential treatment by others.

_____ 6. Boys tend to get more direct instruction from teachers than do girls.

_____ 7. Gender constancy refers to the understanding that gender remains the same across situations.

_____ 8. The simplest hypothesized gender schema is the own-sex schema.

_____ 9. According to gender schema theory, children tend to overinvestigate objects and activities that are associated with the other sex.

_____ 10. There are no obvious differences in male and female infants' behavior or appearance.

_____ 11. Menarche and spermarche are associated with the onset of sexual attraction.

_____ 12. Boys and girls are nearly equivalent in average IQ scores.

_____ 13. Boys' spatial ability has been enhanced over the last 25 years, while girls' spatial ability has remained stable.

_____ 14. Boys' increased vulnerability to attention-related disorders may be due to high levels of androgen exposure during prenatal development.

_____ 15. Boys and girls exhibit similar levels of distress and embarrassment.

_____ 16. Female infants are more distressed than male infants by the "still-face" procedure.

_____ 17. Contrary to stereotypes, boys are no more likely than girls to engage in risky behavior.

_____ 18. Boys tend to be higher than girls in verbal aggression.

_____ 19. Both the level of exposure to aggression and the effect of the exposure differ for males and females.

_____   20.   Whereas girls often engage in behavior that is considered to be appropriate for boys, boys rarely engage in behavior that is considered to be appropriate for girls.

Multiple-Choice Questions

1. Which of the following qualities is considered instrumental?
    A. intelligent
    B. competitive
    C. empathetic
    D. all of the above

2. Children tend to know which gender group they belong to by what age?
    A. 1 year
    B. 18 months
    C. 3 years
    D. 4 years

3. Nine-year-old Kylie is told a story about a female infant who was raised only by males. Kylie then asked to predict what the child will be like when she is 10 years old. Kylie is most likely to predict that the child will exhibit characteristics typical of:
    A. females.
    B. males.
    C. both females and males.
    D. neither females nor males.

4. Evolutionary psychologists would be most interested in which of the following?
    A. gender differences in aggression
    B. societal values and customs
    C. differences in the ways parents structure boys' and girls' living spaces
    D. children's realization of the differences between individuals who have a penis and those who do not

5. In boys, levels of rough-and-tumble play are associated with:
    A. the proportion of cortical white matter.
    B. levels of androgens.
    C. the onset of puberty.
    D. brain size.

6. According to social learning theory, Cheryl, a four-year-old girl, would be LEAST likely to learn by watching the behavior of which of the following people?
    A. Julia, her mother
    B. Matthew, a neighbor boy
    C. Mrs. Delaney, her preschool teacher
    D. Jillian, a girl in her class

7. Which of the following reflects parental socialization of gender-appropriate behavior?
   A. Infants show preferences for toys considered gender-appropriate.
   B. Parents are more responsive to children when they are engaging in sex-appropriate play than when they are engaging in cross-sex play.
   C. Children pay more attention to same-sex models than to opposite-sex models.
   D. all of the above

8. Which of the following is NOT a gender-essentialist statement?
   A. "Boys like trucks."
   B. "Girls do ballet, and boys play soccer."
   C. "Girls like to talk when they are upset."
   D. "The boys in your class are rowdy."

9. Which of the following statements regarding treatment of the sexes in the media is true?
   A. The differences in the representations of males and females in TV are very small.
   B. Portrayals of males and females tend to be less stereotyped than males and females are in reality.
   C. It has changed relatively little over the past three decades.
   D. Any differences in the media tend not to be noticed by young children.

10. In the classroom, gender-role behavior is shaped by:
    A. teachers' tendency to call on boys more than on girls.
    B. differential treatment from teachers for obedient and assertive behaviors.
    C. teachers' tendency to praise boys more than girls.
    D. all of the above.
    E. none of the above.

11. Which of the following lists Kohlberg's stages of the development of gender knowledge in the correct chronological order, from earliest to latest?
    A. gender stability, gender identity, gender constancy
    B. gender identity, gender constancy, gender stability
    C. gender constancy, gender identity, gender stability
    D. gender identity, gender stability, gender constancy

12. Kohlberg's concept of gender identity involves the understanding that:
    A. one is a member of one gender category or another.
    B. gender is consistent even when superficial changes occur.
    C. gender is stable over time.
    D. gender is determined by sex chromosomes.

13. Both cognitive developmental theory and social learning theory explain gendered behavior with which of the following?
  A. imitation of same-sex models
  B. a three-stage process
  C. differential treatment by others
  D. differential expectations of others

14. Which of the following is NOT an effect of gender schemas?
  A. biased processing of information about gender
  B. biased recall of gender information
  C. preference for objects, even unfamiliar ones that are labeled, "for my sex."
  D. All of the above are effects of gender schemas.

15. Which of the following researchers hypothesizes that same-sex play choices originate in sex differences in children's play styles?
  A. Bem
  B. Kohlberg
  C. Maccoby
  D. Geary

16. For the sex differences in psychological variables that have been well documented, the differences between males and females are:
  A. slight.
  B. great.
  C. easily traced to biological differences.
  D. easily traced to socialization.

17. Which of the following is NOT experienced by females?
  A. adrenarche
  B. menarche
  C. spermarche
  D. Neither A nor B are experienced by females.
  E. Neither A nor C are experienced by females.

18. Girls tend to be stronger than boys in:
  A. general intelligence.
  B. mathematical problem solving.
  C. early language development.
  D. all of the above.
  E. none of the above.

19. Males are more likely than females to be diagnosed with:
   A. generalized anxiety disorder.
   B. autism.
   C. post-traumatic stress disorder.
   D. severe depression.

20. Boys' and girls' moral orientation appears to:
   A. diverge during early childhood.
   B. diverge during middle childhood.
   C. diverge during adolescence.
   D. remain nearly the same throughout life.

Essay Questions

Instructions: Answer the following essay questions on a separate sheet of paper.

1. A great deal of research has been directed toward exposing the differences between the ways parents treat their sons and daughters. Discuss at least two ways that parents' treatment of their boys and girls appears to be similar and at least two ways that it has been found to be different.

2. Describe Maccoby's theory of the development of gender differences. Be specific and give supportive examples.

3. Hale and Hailey wish to raise their children as minimally sex-typed as possible. What are three pieces of advice you could offer based on the theories and research presented in this chapter?

4. Describe the evolutionary perspective on gendered behavior. Do you agree with this perspective? Provide at least three arguments to support your view.

5. Describe the stages of Kohlberg's cognitive developmental theory of sex-role development. Give an example of a child at each stage.

Answer Key

Key Term Matching I

1. j	4. o	7. i	10. k	13. b	16. l
2. p	5. d	8. h	11. m	14. g
3. n	6. c	9. a	12. f	15. e

Key Term Matching II

1. e	4. h	7. o	10. i	13. a
2. j	5. f	8. g	11. d	14. n
3. k	6. l	9. b	12. c	15. m

True/False Questions

1. T	6. T	11. F	16. T
2. F	7. T	12. T	17. F
3. T	8. F	13. F	18. T
4. F	9. F	14. T	19. T
5. F	10. T	15. F	20. T

Multiple-Choice Questions

1. B	6. B	11. D	16. A
2. C	7. B	12. A	17. C
3. A	8. D	13. A	18. C
4. A	9. C	14. D	19. B
5. B	10. D	15. C	20. C

CHAPTER 16
Conclusions

Learning Objectives

Following the completion of the study of Chapter 16, you should be able to:

1. Demonstrate an understanding of the theme of nature and nurture by explaining several sources of complexity in the relationship between nature and nurture.

2. Show comprehension of the theme of the active child by discussing four ways in which children contribute to their own development.

3. Explain how development is both continuous and discontinuous at the same time.

4. Convey an understanding of mechanisms of developmental change by identifying specific biological, behavioral, and cognitive change mechanisms.

5. Provide examples of the ways that the sociocultural context shapes development.

6. Demonstrate an understanding of how children become so different from one another by explaining how to determine which individual differences are the crucial ones.

   Convey an appreciation that child-development research can improve children's lives by providing examples of theoretical constructs and empirical findings that can enhance parenting, education, and services for children at risk, and that can improve social policy.

You Should Know:

Theme 1: Nature and Nurture: All Interactions, All the Time *(pg. 606)*

Nature and Nurture Begin Interacting Before Birth
- how prenatal development involves not only nature, but nurture and the interaction between the two as well.
- how teratogenic effects and fetal learning are good examples of this concept.

Infants' Nature Elicits Nurture
- how infants' biological characteristics influence their environments.

287

288 CHAPTER 16   Conclusions

Timing Matters
- how the nature of the individual at the time of an environmental event can influence the impact of the event.
- how sensitive or critical periods are good examples of this concept.

Nature Does Not Reveal Itself All at Once
- how the influence of genetics does not stop at birth.
- how the development of schizophrenia is a good example of this concept.

Everything Influences Everything
- the extent to which the statement "Everything influences everything else" is accurate and why this is the case.

Theme 2: Children Play Active Roles in Their Own Development *(pg. 610)*

Self-Initiated Activity
- how self-initiated activity, including self-locomotion and self-socialization, contributes to children's development.

Active Interpretation of Experience
- how children's attempts to understand the world and their subjective interpretations of their experiences influence their development.

Self-Regulation
- how children's regulation of their emotions, behavior, activities, etc. contributes to their development.

Eliciting Reactions from Other People
- how children's characteristics and behavior elicit the behaviors of their parents and peers.
- how the negative cycles sometimes experienced by adolescents and their parents are good examples of this concept.

Theme 3: Development Is Both Continuous and Discontinuous *(pg. 613)*

Continuity/Discontinuity of Individual Differences
- how continuous individual differences tend to be over time.
- what accounts for the continuity of individual differences.

Continuity/Discontinuity of Overall Development: The Question of Stages

- the assumptions of stage theories.

- the extent to which stage theories can accurately capture development.

- how one's focus influences whether development appears to be continuous or discontinuous.

Theme 4: Mechanisms of Developmental Change *(pg. 616)*

Biological Change Mechanisms

- how brain development illustrates the complexity of change at the biological level.

Behavioral Change Mechanisms

- how behavioral change mechanisms, including both basic learning mechanisms and social learning, facilitate learning.

- some examples of each of these behavioral change mechanisms.

Cognitive Change Mechanisms

- how general information-processing mechanisms and domain-specific learning mechanisms facilitate developmental change.

- examples of each of these cognitive change mechanisms.

Theme 5: The Sociocultural Context Shapes Development *(pg. 621)*

Growing Up in Societies with Different Values

- how cultural values and practices can underlie a variety of variations across cultures, even in areas that would appear to be biological, such as rate of development.

- the ways in which cultural values exert their influence and some examples of these modes of influence.

Growing Up in Different Times and Places

- how historical changes influence children's development.

Growing Up in Different Circumstances Within a Society

- how differences in economic circumstances, family relationships, and peer groups can lead to differences in children's development, even for children growing up in the same time and place.

Theme 6: How Do Children Become So Different from One Another? *(pg. 625)*

Introduction

- what three properties are important in determining whether a dimension of individual differences is considered important.

Breadth of Individual Differences at a Given Time

- what types of individual differences are associated with a broad range of other variables.

Stability over Time

- how the stability of genes and the stability of environment contribute to the stability of many individual differences.

Predicting Future Individual Differences on Other Dimensions

- what contributes to the long-term relations between some individual differences and other important variables.

Determinants of Individual Differences

- the extent to which genes contribute to differences among individuals and how the influence of genetics changes over the course of development.
- the extent to which experience contributes to differences among individuals.

Theme 7: Child-Development Research Can Improve Children's Lives *(pg. 628)*

Implications for Parenting

- what principles of good parenting are suggested by developmental theory and research.

Implications for Education

- what principles of good education are suggested by the four major theories of cognitive development.

Implications for Helping Children at Risk

- what principles are suggested for helping children at risk for developmental problems.
- some examples of these principles at work.

Improving Social Policy

- how knowledge of developmental research can help us make better-informed decisions about a variety of social policy issues.
- some examples of the impact of research on policy.

True/False Questions

Instructions: Indicate whether each item is true or false.

_____ 1. Abilities that are present at birth are rarely influenced by fetal learning.

_____ 2. The influence of environmental forces tends to be the same across individuals.

_____ 3. Self-initiated activity includes, among other things, self-locomotion, self-socialization, and use of language.

_____ 4. Physically attractive babies tend to evoke more positive parenting than do other babies.

_____ 5. The degree of continuity of individual differences tends to be higher in social, emotional, and personal development than it is in intellectual development.

_____ 6. Identifying developmental milestones is important, but it is difficult to precisely determine when a given competency develops.

_____ 7. Synaptogenesis is an example of a social learning mechanism.

_____ 8. Habituation must be learned and thus only contributes to development some time following its acquisition.

_____ 9. Cultural values can influence a wide variety of domains, from motor skill development to intellectual development to social development.

_____ 10. In countries with a low degree of economic inequality, being from an affluent family offers children no cognitive or social advantage.

_____ 11. An individual difference is considered particularly interesting to developmentalists if it occurs for a brief period of time and in a sporadic manner.

_____ 12. Although self-esteem does not meet the requirements of an important individual difference variable, developmentalists find it conceptually interesting and thus often study it.

_____ 13. Child-development research can inform parents about which decisions are likely to have a long-term impact and which decisions are not likely to matter in the long run.

_____ 14. Developmental research has provided a great deal of evidence about the importance of timing.

Multiple-Choice Questions

1. Which of the following is an example of the interplay between nature and nurture before birth?
    A. The genetics of the fetus partially determines the effect of teratogens on prenatal development.
    B. The hormones released by the fetus change the prenatal environment, which then influences the fetus.
    C. The food that the mother eats while pregnant influences newborn taste preferences.
    D. All of the above are examples of the interplay between nature and nurture before birth

2. Which of the following is NOT an example of a self-initiated activity that allows children to actively influence their environment?
    A. language
    B. walking
    C. attractiveness
    D. looking preferences
    E. taste preferences

3. Focusing on which of the following generally makes development appear more continuous?
    A. specific tasks and processes rather than broad domains
    B. behaviors rather than underlying processes
    C. smaller time frames rather than larger time frames
    D. both A and C
    E. all of the above
    F. none of the above

4. Which of the following is NOT a mechanism of developmental change?
    A. history
    B. biology
    C. social learning
    D. metacognition

5. Japanese culture's value on hiding negative emotions could play a role in differences between U.S. and Japanese children's:
    A. peer relations.
    B. emotional regulation.
    C. moral development.
    D. aggression.
    E. development of all of the above.

6. Which of the following is NOT a key reason why social competence is considered an important individual difference?
    A. Socially competent children tend to become socially competent adolescents who tend to become socially competent adults.
    B. Social competence in childhood predicts future outcomes, such as self esteem.
    C. Social competence has its basis in genetics.
    D. Social competence has a variety of concurrent associations, such as the number of friends a child has.
    E. All of the above are key reasons why social competence is considered an important individual difference.

7. Which of the following is NOT a valid conclusion to be drawn from this course when thinking about the implications of developmental psychology for education and social policy?
    A. Most developmental problems stem from one major source, so it is important that we find that source before intervening with children.
    B. Timing of interventions is crucial; in general, the earlier children receive help, the more successful the outcome.
    C. Designing treatments for undesirable behavior is best done by attending to both the biological and environmental factors that are involved.
    D. All of the above are valid conclusions.
    E. None of the above is a valid conclusion.

THE LEARNING CENTRE
TOWER HAMLETS COLLEGE
ARBOUR SQUARE
LONDON E1 0PS

Essay Questions

Instructions: Answer the following essay questions on a separate sheet of paper.

1. Choose a domain of development – cognitive, moral, social, language, physical, etc. – and describe three ways in which development in this domain is continuous and three ways in which it is discontinuous. Do the specifics of what you are focusing on change your perception as to whether development in the domain is generally continuous or generally discontinuous?

2. Thinking about the extent to which many individual differences remain stable over time, describe three reasons why self-esteem demonstrates high stability over time. Be sure to provide examples of each.

3. Describe three ways in which children's self-initiated activity actively influences their environment. Be sure to provide examples of each.

4. Think about your own childhood, the development of a particular trait, or your parents' parenting practices. Describe three things you have learned in this course that have influenced your perceptions or memories.

Answer Key

True/False Questions

1. F	6. T	11. F
2. F	7. F	12. F
3. T	8. F	13. T
4. T	9. T	14. T
5. F	10. F	

Multiple-Choice Questions

1. D	5. E
2. C	6. C
3. F	7. A
4. A	

Withdrawn

Tower Hamlets College
Learning Centre
105674

Withdrawn

19.99

Study Guide

19.99